A
Southern Woman's
Story

A
Southern Woman's
Story

Life in Confederate Richmond

by
PHOEBE YATES PEMBER

Including unpublished letters written from
the Chimborazo Hospital

Edited by
BELL IRVIN WILEY

McCOWAT-MERCER PRESS, INC.
Monographs, Sources and Reprints in Southern History
Jackson, Tennessee

1959

TABLE OF CONTENTS

ILLUSTRATIONS

Phoebe Yates Pember

Mrs. Jefferson Davis

Chimborazo Hospital, Richmond

Dr. Samuel Preston Moore, Surgeon General, CSA

Dr. James B. McCaw, Chimborazo Hospital

General R. S. Ripley, CSA

Mrs. Arthur F. Hopkins

Henry S. Foote, Congressman from Tennessee, CSA

A patient dictates a letter

"A Hospital Rat"

The Whiskey Barrel, our hero

Home-made playing cards

General Jeremy F. Gilmer, Chief Engineer—CSA

General Wade Hampton, CSA

Confederate attack at Battle of Crater

Wounded soldiers in Richmond Streets

Agnes Lee, daughter of R. E. Lee

Women making clothes for soldiers

Mrs. Philip Phillips, Phoebe's sister

"No one slept during that night of horror . . ."

Union Army entering Richmond

Destruction in Richmond

Negroes greet Federals on their arrival

Ex-slaves collect spoils among ruins

A group of Pember's friends after the war

Painting by Malcolm Thurgood, Austin Texas, based
on a photograph provided by Miss Fanny Phillips

Phoebe Yates Pember

"Well," said a poor wounded fellow when told by the ward-master that I was matron of the hospital, "I always did think this government was a confounded sell and now I am sure of it, when they put such a little fool to manage such a big hospital as this."

Mrs. Jefferson Davis

*"The military men in the highest posts are unacquainted with Lee's plans.
However Mrs. Davis gives out . . . that Lee has not moved from Culpeper."*

Chimborazo Hospital, Richmond, Virginia. Reputedly the largest hospital in the South during Phoebe Pember's connection with it. *"How frightened and nervous I feel concerning the step I am about to take."*

Dr. Samuel Preston Moore,
Surgeon General,
CSA

"The old gentleman was very urbane, even making one or two grim jokes, and handed me not only permission to leave (for a rest from hospital duties) but the necessary transportation."

Dr. James B. McCaw,
Surgeon-in-Chief,
Chimborazo Hospital

"He was energetic—capable—skillful. A man with ready oil to pour upon troubled waters . . . Wisely he decided to have an educated and efficient woman at the head of his hospital."

Henry S. Foote,
Confederate Congressman from
Tennessee

*"I wrote out a memorial for increase in
pay and sent it to old Foote, who I knew
would be glad of any opportunity to hear
himself talk on any subject."*

Mrs. Arthur F. Hopkins,
*"the Florence Nightingale of the
South"*

*"I saw Mrs. Hopkins a week ago . . .
(at) the Alabama Hospital. . .She was
full . . . of herself and her duties and I
did not stay long."*

General R. S. Ripley, CSA

*". . . in blockade running . . . Ripley has
made a million they say . . ."*

A Patient Dictates a Letter

*"My dear Mammy: I hope this finds you well, as it leaves me well, and I hope
that I shall git a furlough Christmas . . ."*

THE HOSPITAL RAT.

"Shut! Shut the door," he shamm'd fatigue, and said:
"Tie up the knocker—say I'm sick! I'm dead!
I'll take your physic, but not take the field:
On this point, courage, for I never yield.
I'll die first! (in the wards,) and paintin scrawls
With desperate charcoal on the darkened walls
All my great efforts, Sir, to help the cause,
And thus obtain what all men seek, applause!
[Giles Scroggins' Ghost.

George Dunn & Comp'y, Publishers, Richmond, Va.

As the Federals took over Richmond, *"beds in which paralyzed, rheumatic and helpless patients had laid for months were empty. The miracles of the New Testament had been re-enacted. The lame, the halt and the blind had been cured."*

The Hospital Rat

"Shut! Shut the door," he shamm'd fatigue, and said:
"Tie up the knocker—say I'm sick! I'm dead!
I'll take your physic, but not take the field:
On this point, courage, for I never yield.
I'll die first! (in the wards,) and paint in scrawls
With desperate charcoal on the darkened walls
All my great efforts, Sir, to help the cause,
And thus obtain what all men seek, applause!

Giles Scruggins' Ghost

The Whiskey Barrel

"The monthly barrel was an institution and a very important one. Indeed, if it is necessary to have a hero for this matter-of-fact narrative, the whiskey barrel will have to step forward and make his bow."

From Richmond City Directory, 1869

Home-made Playing Cards made during the War by John Hill Hewitt of Georgia

"Playing cards—the greatest comfort to alleviate the tedium of their sick life—were difficult to get a substitute for, so that the original packs had a hard time . . . the corners in a particularly disreputable condition . . . the soldiers took a lesson and rounded the corners . . . A pack of cards after four years' use in a Southern hospital was beyond criticism."

General Jeremy F. Gilmer,
Chief Engineer, CSA

*"I shall lose very kind and devoted friends
by Davis appointing Gilmer a Major
General and sending him to Charleston.
I have spent every evening with them
for five months."*

General Wade Hampton, CSA

*"General Hampton was the Mont-
rose of the Southern Army, he who
could make any cause famous with
his pen and glorious with his
sword."*

Confederate Attack on Negro Troops, Battle of
Crater, July 31, 1864

*"After that time the sentiment changed . . . The wounded
brought in from that fight . . . showed me the locks of their
muskets to which the blood and hair still clung, when after
firing, without waiting to re-load, they had clenched the
barrels and fought hand to hand."*

Drawing by William L. Sheppard from Battles
and Leaders of the Civil War, 1887

Wounded Soldiers in the Streets of Richmond

*"The pavement . . . would be crowded with wounded men just brought in
. . . on stretchers . . . or laid on a thin blanket . . . Women passing . . . would
put down their basket or bundle . . . and going from sufferer to sufferer, try
to alleviate the pain, change the uneasy posture and allay the thirst."*

From T. C. DeLeon, Belles, Beaux
and Brains of the 60's

Agnes Lee, Daughter of Robert E. Lee

*"When the daughter of our
general had devoted much
time and care to a sick man
. . . her companion, to rouse
him told him that Miss Lee
was his nurse. 'Lee, Lee?' he
said. 'There are some Lees
down in Mississippi who
keep a tavern there. Is she
one of them Lees'?"*

Southern Women Making Clothes for Soldiers

"The women of the South . . . incited the men to struggle in support of their views, and whether right or wrong, sustained them nobly to the end. They were the first to rebel—the last to succumb."

Mrs. Philip Phillips

"Dear Sister E . . . Do give my kindest remembrances to all your household and write me soon. My greatest pleasure is the letters I get."

"No one slept during that night of horror . . .

Daylight dawned upon a wreck of destruction and desolation. From the highest point of Church hill and Libby hill, the eye could range over the whole extent of the city and country—the fire had not abated, and the burning bridges were adding their flame and smoke to the scene."

Union Army Entering Richmond, April 3, 1865

*"They were well mounted, well accoutered, well fed—a rare sight in Southern
streets—the advance of that vaunted army that for four years had so hopelessly
knocked at the gates of the Southern Confederacy."*

Remnants of Destruction in Occupied Richmond

"The warehouses and tobacco manufactories were fired, cummunicating the flames to the adjacent houses and shops . . . The armory, not intended to be burnt, either caught accidentally or was fired by mistake, the shells exploding and filling the air with hissing sounds of horror."

Negroes Who Greeted the Federals on their Arrival in Richmond

"The colored population shouted and cheered them on their way."

Ex-Slaves Collect Spoils among the Richmond Ruins

"People who . . . were wealthy the day previously looked around in vain for wherewithal to buy a loaf of bread."

Group taken at White Sulphur Springs
(Standing) Left to Right – Mrs. H. H. Ware, Genl. J. S. Preston, Miss Mary Custis Lee, Genl. J. E. Johnston
(Sitting) Mrs. J. E. Johnston, Genl. J. F. Gilmer, Mrs. McLean, Genl. Custis Lee, Mrs. McKim, Mrs. Gilmer.

Some of Phoebe Pember's Friends As They Appeared After the War

INTRODUCTION

A PRETTY MATRON making her rounds in a Richmond hospital in 1862 was asked by a patient: "Kin you write me a letter?" The question was put to her by a rustic Reb from Georgia, whom the matron described as "lean, yellow, attenuated, with wispy strands of hair hanging over his high, thin cheek bones" and with finger-nails so long neglected that they were like claws. After exacting from the sick Reb a promise that he would have his hair and nails cut, the matron seated herself beside the bed and started a message to "my dear Mammy."

Before the first paragraph was completed the dictation bogged down and the soldier's mind "seemed to be going around in a circle." The matron laid aside her pen and asked the patient some questions about his family, friends and recent army experiences. She then proceeded to fill up four pages with the information thus obtained. When the letter was finished she read it aloud to the attentive patient.

"Did *I* say all that?" he asked.

"I think you did," replied the amanuensis.

After a long silence during which his face registered admiration and astonishment, the soldier quietly asked: "Are you married?"

"I am not. At least I am a widow," came the reply.

Then, in the words of the matron: "He rose still higher in bed. He pushed away desperately the tangled hay on

1

his brow. A faint color fluttered over the hollow cheeks, and stretching out a long piece of bone with a talon attached he gently touched my arm, and with constrained voice whispered mysteriously: 'You wait'."

The woman to whom this odd proposal was addressed was Phoebe Yates Pember and the scene was the division of Chimborazo Hospital over which she presided as matron from 1862 to 1865. The richness of the letter-writing incident and the rare artistry with which the story is told, make it easy to understand why Mrs. Pember's book about her hospital experiences is rated as one of the very best Confederate memoirs. The late Douglas Southall Freeman stated: *"A Southern Woman's Story* . . . would be heartbreaking were it not told with an odd humor. She wrote as she talked, always to the point." Her account of the letter-writing experience drew from Freeman the comment: "Surely this reveals as much of Southern character, male and female, and explains as much of the war as does any page of Mr. Davis's or any ream of Mr. Stephens'. If historians have lapsed since Mrs. Pember's day in realistic treatment of the war, the fault assuredly is not hers."

The excellence and charm of *A Southern Woman's Story* are attributable primarily to the fact that the author was a remarkable woman. She was born into a prosperous and cultured Jewish family of Charleston, South Carolina, on August 18, 1823. Her father, Jacob Clavius Levy, was described by one of his great-granddaughters as "a gentleman of leisure and quite literary." Her mother, Fanny Yates, a native of England, was said to have been "a marvel of sprightliness" even after she celebrated her eightieth birthday. In the 1850's Jacob Levy changed his residence from Charleston to Savannah.

Phoebe was the fourth of six daughters in the Levy household.* An elder sister, Eugenia, married Philip Phillips, an Alabama congressman from 1853 to 1855 and subsequently a Washington attorney. During the Civil War Mrs. Phillips, who was an outspoken Rebel, became the subject of international comment when she clashed with General Benjamin F. Butler at New Orleans. Arrested on the charge of laughing as the remains of a Federal officer were borne past her residence, and despite her claim that the merriment was occasioned by a children's party in her house and not the funeral procession on the street, she was haled before the stern commander of the occupying forces. When she refused to apologize, Butler heatedly denounced her as not just "a vulgar woman of the town, but an uncommonly vulgar one," banished her to Ship Island, and forbade her to communicate with anyone save him and her maid.** Before the general sent her away, she demonstrated the spunk for which she, Phoebe, and other members of the family were famous. According to T. C. DeLeon, when Eugenia Phillips was told by Butler that she was to be sent to Ship Island she blandly replied: "It has one advantage over the city, sir; you will not be there."

---

*The children of J. C. and Fanny Yates Levy were:

1. Henrietta—born May 30, 1818. Married Octavus Cohen. Children: Fanny, Georgina Bryant and Octavus S.

2. Eugenia—born Oct. 24, 1819. Married Philip Phillips. Children: Clavius, Fanny, Caroline (Lena), Eugene, John Walker, John Randolph, Emma Louise, William Hallett, Philip Lee.

3. Martha Sarah—born April 27, 1821.

4. Phoebe—born Aug. 18, 1823. Married Thomas Pember.

5. Samuel Yates—born Sept. 14, 1827.

6. Emma—born Oct. 13, 1832. Married S. Prioleau Hamilton. Children: Emma, James and another son.

7. Fanny—Jan. 1, 1840. Married George Repplier.

**An unpublished account of the arrest and imprisonment, written by Mrs. Phillips after the war, for her children, is filed with the Philip Phillips Papers in the Manuscripts Division of the Library of Congress.

When informed that Ship Island was a Yellow Fever station she retorted: "It is fortunate that neither the fever nor General Butler is contagious."

Nothing is known of Phoebe's schooling. She probably studied under private tutors and she may have followed the example of Varina Howell and other daughters of upper class Southerners by attending a Northern finishing school. In any event, her war-time letters and her reminiscences indicate that she was a well-educated woman.

Some time before the outbreak of the Civil War, Phoebe married Thomas Pember of Boston. After the marriage Pember contracted tuberculosis and moved South in the hope of improving his health. He died at Aiken, South Carolina, on July 9, 1861, at the age of thirty-six. After her husband's death Phoebe went to live with her parents. In 1862, if not earlier, the family "refugeed" to Marietta, Georgia.

Mrs. Pember's war-time letters indicate that she was not happy in Marietta. Living with relatives gave rise to frictions, and the inactivity must have been trying to one of Phoebe's energy and ability. In November, 1862, acquaintance with Mrs. George W. Randolph, wife of the Confederate Secretary of War, brought her an offer to serve as matron in Chimborazo Hospital. Despite some misgivings as to the wisdom of her action, she immediately accepted the offer and set out for the Confederate capital.

Chimborazo Hospital, where she reported for duty in December, 1862, was a sprawling institution perched on a high hill near the western boundary of Richmond. It began receiving patients early in 1862 and was subsequently expanded to provide for the increasing hordes of sick and wounded that poured into the Confederate capital. It eventually numbered 150 wards, each normally under the care of an assistant surgeon and housed in a separate one-story building thirty feet wide and one hundred feet long with a capacity of forty to sixty patients. The wards were grouped into five divisions, or "hospitals," each presided over by a surgeon-in-charge. The surgeon-in-chief of the whole establishment was Dr. James B. McCaw, whom Douglas Southall Freeman characterized as "one of the great men of the South."

A total of 76,000 patients were treated at Chimborazo during the course of the Civil War. It was reputed to be the largest military hospital in the world up to that time, the next in size being Lincoln Hospital in Washington, D. C., which cared for a total of 46,000 patients and Scutari Hospital in the Crimea which treated from 30,000 to 40,000.

In a letter of November 29, 1862, to her sister, Mrs. Pember stated that she was "to take charge of one of the hospitals at Richmond" and certain references in her memoir leave the impression that her supervisory responsibilities extended throughout Chimborazo. But records in the National Archives indicate that she was chief matron of the institution's second division, which usually appears in reports as "Hospital No. 2."

Apparently she was the first matron appointed at Chimborazo and, like other women who undertook the nursing of soldiers during the Civil War, she encountered considerable opposition when she entered into what at that time was regarded as a domain reserved for males. The general reaction to her arrival was pungently expressed by one of the ward surgeons who in a loud whisper informed a friend "in a tone of ill-concealed disgust that *one of them had come*."

As her associates of both sexes soon learned, this dynamic little woman from the deep South was not one who could be pushed around. She ignored the opposition based on prejudice and pitched into the more tangible obstacles with a zest and determination that accomplished wonders. No steps had been taken to provide her with living quarters (which for a time were at the hospital), office and other essential facilities. These deficiencies, under her spirited urging, were quickly remedied. The next move was to obtain the help and provisions required for feeding patients who were on special diets and performing other services for which she was responsible. She was successful in all of her initial activities, with one major exception.

The exception was the dispensing of whiskey. Confederate law provided that spirituous liquors required by hospitals should be entrusted to the matrons. When Mrs. Pember sought to implement the law by sending in a formal requisition for the monthly supply of one barrel that was allotted to her division, the surgeon-in-charge politely refused to deliver the whiskey. He was strongly supported by his assistants and other members of the administrative hierarchy. But Mrs. Pember cited the law sustaining her request and the whiskey was delivered to her charge.

This did not end the difficulty; indeed, Mrs. Pember's first triumph was only the beginning of a long and bitterly waged contest for the control of a commodity which was always in great demand and which eventually became a symbol of authority in a tussle between the male and female contingents of the hospital staff.

Some of the "small fry," as Mrs. Pember called the assistant surgeons and their helpers, sought to get even with the matron by flooding her office with petty requests couched in official language. These she usually met by simply ignoring them. More serious was the constant complaint of the patients that they did not receive the whiskey prescribed by the doctors and dispensed from the matron's supply. In an effort to stop the leakage Mrs. Pember employed three women nurses and entrusted to them the delivery of liquor to the patients. She selected the new assistants from the lower classes rather than more prominent groups, on the ground that the less privileged women would be amenable to supervision. The experiment was a complete failure. The three female helpers, far from submitting readily to authority, openly defied the matron, one by stating that as a "decent woman" she was "not going anywhere in a place where a man sat up on his bed in a shirt," and the other two by appropriating for their own comfort space and furniture reserved for the patients. To cap the climax one of the women got thoroughly intoxicated from the whiskey that she was supposed to be giving to the patients and had to be hauled away from the hospital in the matron's ambulance.

Conflict over control of the whiskey did not abate with departure of the women nurses. Every conceivable strategem was used by some of the surgeons to circumvent the matron's determined efforts to see that liquor was given only to persons for whom it was intended and in authorized quantities. Mrs. Pember was only partially successful in defeating these ruses. One doctor—a contract surgeon who had been a bartender in a Georgia tavern—after prescribing a pint of liquor for a patient and having the quantity reduced on Mrs. Pember's appeal to the chief surgeon to the authorized dosage of two to four ounces, retaliated by demanding absurd reports on previous whiskey issues to individual patients. When she ignored one of these demands, her tormenter made an official complaint against her which eventually reached the Secretary of War. This cabinet officer, who was a personal friend of Mrs. Pember, was amused by the protest; and the surgeon who originated it was eventually relieved of his position.

In 1863 Mrs. Pember, utilizing transportation provided by the hospital, began to spend her evenings in the city. For a time she had quarters at the residence of the Secretary of War, but during most of her sojourn in the capital she appears to have lived in a room rented from a Mrs. Skinner.

Absence from the hospital during off-duty hours made life much more tolerable for the matron. Her intelligence, beauty, vivaciousness, and social standing made her a welcome member in the capital's most exclusive social gatherings. T. C. DeLeon, who has been appropriately called "the Confederate St. Simon," tells in *Belles, Beaux and Brains of the Sixties* of a charade given by Mrs. George W. Randolph early in 1863 in which Phoebe Pember, "a belle and early a widow," cleverly represented Laurence Sterne's *Widow Wadman* to help act the word "penitent." Further insight into Mrs. Pember's personality and attractiveness is afforded by DeLeon's comment that the "brisk and brilliant matron" of Chimborazo had "a will of steel under a suave refinement" and that "her pretty, almost Creole accent covered the power to ring in *defi* on occasion." He added that "the friction of these attributes against bumptiousness or young authority made the hospital the field of many 'fusses' and more fun."

Social activities had only limited appeal for Mrs. Pember during the war years. Her consuming interest from December, 1862, through Appomattox was the care of the sick and wounded who filled her wards at Chimborazo. The battles for recognition and authority that she fought and won were conducted mainly for her patients.

And there can be no doubt that her charges benefited from her diligent and dauntless oversight.

A Southern Woman's Story is valuable primarily for what it tells of conditions in a major Confederate hospital. One of the author's most notable attributes was her forth-rightness; and the story that she tells does not reflect great credit upon those charged with the care of Confederate sick and wounded. Even though Chimborazo was located in the capital and was headed by a respected, high-minded surgeon, its administration, like that of the Con-federate Government, suffered from red tape, incompe-tency of key officials and internal strife.*

Some of the doctors rendered outstanding service in spite of enormous difficulty. But dearth of qualified per-sonnel and haphazard selection resulted in the appoint-ment of many men to surgeons' positions who were sadly deficient both in character and in professional ability. Some had a fondness for the bottle that interfered with the effective discharge of their duties. Mrs. Pember cites one case of a soldier whose ankle had been crushed in a railroad accident falling into the hands of a surgeon so befuddled by liquor that he set and bandaged the sound leg instead of the broken one. The victim's subsequent complaint of pain in the untreated leg was attributed to sympathetic suffering and a sedative was administered. By the time the drunken doctor's mistake was discovered complications had set in and the patient eventually died.

Much of the suffering and death at Chimborazo was unavoidable, owing to shortages of personnel, medicine,

---

*Reports, filed in the National Archives, of Officers of the Day, Chimborazo Hospital No. 2, for the period Oct. 17, 1864-March 28, 1865, show that fuel was frequently inadequate, causing much discomfort to the patients; that food was often skimpy in quantity and inferior in quality; that soap was sometimes unavailable in necessary amounts; that bandages were re-used without being cleansed; that clothing of patients was sometimes dirty; and that toilets occasionally were filthy.

food and equipment, and the relatively undeveloped
state of scientific knowledge. The recounting of instances
of patients who at first were hearty and hopeful—and
who, if they could have enjoyed the benefits of present-
day treatment, would have speedily recovered—suffering
a reverse, slipping into decline, turning their faces to the
wall and dying, gives to Mrs. Pember's book a strain of
pathos and tragedy.

After Fredericksburg, the matron was summoned to the
bed of a mortally wounded boy soldier. She offered him
food, drink, lighter covering and a softer pillow, but
these suggestions he turned aside with a shake of the head.

"I want Perry," he said. Further inquiry revealed that
Perry was an intimate associate of camp and battlefield.
After much searching Mrs. Pember found Perry in a
nearby camp, took him to the hospital in her ambulance,
and led him to the side of his wounded comrade. The
boy had fallen asleep but he roused just as Perry settled
down beside his bunk. A smile of recognition illumined
the pale face. " 'Perry,' he cried, 'Perry,' and not another
word but with one last effort he threw himself into his
friend's arms, the radiant eyes closed, but the smile still
remained—he was dead."

Even more heart-rending is the case of Fisher as
recorded by Mrs. Pember. This young soldier had won
the admiration and affection of all those who came in
contact with him by the patience and cheerfulness mani-
fested during a ten-month convalescence from a hip
wound. On the night following his first success in walking from one end of the ward to the other, Fisher cried
out with pain as he turned over in his bed. Examination
revealed a small stream of blood spurting from his wound;
a splintered bone apparently had cut an artery. Mrs.
Pember stopped the blood flow with her finger and sent

for the surgeon. The doctor promptly concluded that the severed artery was too deeply imbedded in the fleshy part of the thigh to be repaired.

When informed of the hopelessness of his plight the young man gave the matron his mother's address and then asked: "How long can I live?"

"Only as long as I keep my finger upon this artery," Mrs. Pember replied.

Then followed a silence broken by the simple remark, "You can let go—."

"But I could not," wrote Mrs. Pember in her memoir. "Not if my own life had trembled in the balance. Hot tears rushed to my eyes, a surging sound to my ears, and a deathly coldness to my lips."

"The pang of obeying him was spared me," she added, "and for the first and last time during the trials that surrounded me for four years, I fainted away."

*   *   *   *   *   *

Mrs. Pember's narrative throws much light on the character and customs of the lowly folk who comprised the great bulk of the Southern population and provided most of the fighters for the Confederate armies. Their manner of talk is illustrated by a standard response of new patients to inquiries about the progress of an indecisive battle: "We druv 'em nowhere"; and a Tar Heel's recipe for sour soup: "You jist put a crock of buttermilk on the fire, and let it come to a bile; then mix up the yaller of an egg with some corn flour . . . then punch off pieces of the dough and bile them with the soup, with lots of pepper and salt."

Some of the rustic and semi-literate patients who came under her observation were gifted persons who with better opportunity might have achieved a considerably higher standing in society. Aesthetic aspirations and tendencies were made apparent to the matron by "little poetical effusions" which were often slipped under her door. And at Chimborazo, as in all other hospitals, some of the convalescents displayed much artistic talent by carving figures of all sorts from wood, bone and other available materials.

By no means all of the lowly people whom Phoebe Pember encountered were admirable. Chimborazo had its share of malingerers, better known as "hospital rats." One of these, a ruffian named Wilson, tried to force the matron to give whiskey to him and some associates when the Confederates evacuated Richmond. He called her an indecent name and seized her by the shoulder, but the ominous click of a small pistol which she had concealed in her pocket caused him to beat a hasty though defiant retreat.*

Most of the difficulties which Mrs. Pember had with her less privileged patients were of a minor character, such as complaints about food, failure to observe hospital routine, and squabbles with other convalescents. State rights, the *bete noire* of the Confederate Government, lifted its ugly head in the hospital wards and gave rise to much annoying friction. When Mrs. Pember attempted to improve the lot of Marylanders, cut off from their homes and hence unable to receive delicacies from relatives, patients from other states, and especially those from

---

*An interesting case of malingering is described by the following letter, in the National Archives, of S. E. Habersham, Surgeon-in-Charge, Chimborazo Hospital No. 2, to Brig. Gen. John M. Winder, no date, but December, 1862: "Gen'l

In compliance with your verbal order to me yesterday I have ordered Dennis Fitzgerald [Co. K, 20th Ga. Regt.] to report to you this morning. He has been in this Hospital since its organization and has made constant application for a discharge—he has many complaints, none of which are real, and finding it impossible to keep him from his bottle, I returned him yesterday as fit for duty."

Virginia, indignantly charged her with favoritism. And inmates from the deep South resented anything which might be construed as partiality for Virginians. Then, among soldiers of the same state, tensions existed between the low-country and the up-country groups. Much of the inter-state and inter-sectional recrimination was mere chaff, aimed at relieving boredom. But some of it, as Mrs. Pember discovered, was an expression of real jealousy and deep resentment.

One of the characteristics demonstrated by the humble folk was a strong attachment to their families. Sick and wounded rustics were especially susceptible to nostalgia, and as Phoebe Pember astutely observed, "the homesickness which wrings the heart and impoverishes the blood killed many a brave soldier."

When circumstances permitted, the homefolk came thronging into the wards to visit their soldier relations. Sometimes these visitors displayed more persistence than judgement, extending their stay to lengths that interfered with the work of the staff and inconvenienced and endangered the patients. Mrs. Pember records the instance of a Mrs. Daniells who made a prolonged visit to her sick husband and then refused to depart when he recovered and went back to his regiment. Her excuse was the desire to be on hand in case Daniells should be wounded in a battle that was thought to be imminent.

Mrs. Daniells stayed on, and within a week her husband was back in the hospital with a wound in his neck. A month later Mrs. Pember was summoned to Daniells' bed; and she beheld there, not the injured Reb, but Mrs. Daniells, and by her side a baby just two hours old!

Most of the lowly people who had husbands, fathers, sons, and brothers in the hospital were unable to attend personally to the needs of their ailing kin. But they evi-

denced their unselfishness and devotion by laboriously
writing letters and at great sacrifice sending boxes filled
with bedding, clothing and food to make more tolerable
the lot of their loved ones. The sick and wounded men
to whom these tokens of affection were directed proved
the worthiness of the masses whom they represented by
the politeness and kindness which they showed to each
other and to the hospital staff and by the patience and
cheerfulness with which they endured adversity and
suffering. Mrs. Pember, who was an aristocrat ever conscious of her status, developed a deep admiration of the
common soldiers and the class from which they came.
She wrote to a friend that the enlisted men as a rule were
more courteous than the officers. And her memoir contains
the following eloquent tribute to plain civilians:

> "These letters making inquiries concerning patients from
> relatives at home, directed oftener to my office than my name,
> came in numbers and were queer mixtures of ignorance, bad
> grammar, worse spelling and simple feeling. However absurd
> the style, the love that filled them chastened and purified
> them."

Another interesting sidelight on the common soldiers
afforded by Mrs. Pember's account is their changing attitude toward the war and their opponents. "In no instance,
up to a certain period," she states, "did I hear of any
remark that savored of personal hatred. They fought for
a cause and against a power, and would speak in depreciation of a [Federal] corps or brigade; but 'they fit us and
we fit them' was the whole story generally, and till the
blowing up of the mine at Petersburg, there was a gay,
insouciant style in their descriptions of the war scenes
passing under their observation."

After the Petersburg fight of July 30, 1864, this
detached, impersonal attitude seemed to be supplanted by
a sense of earnest commitment and a feeling of deep

hatred. Mrs. Pember attributed this change partly to resentment of the breaching of the Confederate lines by a mine as a "mean trick" and partly to the fact that Negro troops were used to exploit the advantage gained by the explosion. The Crater battle marked the first instance in which Negro soldiers were used in combat on a large scale in Virginia. And there can be no doubt that Federal employment of colored soldiers, most of whom were ex-slaves, infuriated Johnny Rebs and deepened their antipathy toward their foes.

*   *   *   *   *   *

A Southern Woman's Story gives revealing insight into many other aspects of Confederate life. The blighting effects of the twin evils of scarcity and inflation are effectively portrayed in Mrs. Pember's account of her difficulty in making a living in war-time Richmond. The discomforts, inconveniences and peril of travel late in the Confederate period are vividly represented by the detailed description that she gives of her trip to Georgia in October, 1864. The "mad gaiety" into which the people of Richmond plunged themselves in the last winter of the war, and which J. B. Jones, Mary Boykin Chesnut, and others reported in their diaries, is faithfully depicted by Mrs. Pember and correctly interpreted by her as a frenzied effort to squeeze a few drops of pleasure from an existence that was known to be nearing an end.

When the end finally came in April, 1865, Mrs. Pember stayed at her post so that her patients might be cared for during the transition from Confederate to Federal control. This proved to be a trying and perilous period, by far the most critical of her war-time experiences. She met the emergency with a resourcefulness and courage which reflected great credit on her as an individual and on a group which she and countless other Confederate women clearly demonstrated were not the "weaker sex." When at last her responsibilities had been fully discharged she returned to Georgia. During the post-war years she devoted much time to travel, both in America and abroad. She died in Pittsburgh on March 4, 1913. Her remains were brought back to Savannah and buried beside those of her husband in Laurel Grove Cemetery.

Mrs. Pember wrote *A Southern Woman's Story* sometime between 1865 and 1879. She apparently wrote from memory though she probably had at hand some papers and documents bearing on her war-time experience. Comparison of the memoir with the few extant letters that she wrote during her hospital connection indicates that her narrative is generally accurate. She seems to have attempted in a few instances to conceal the identity of persons with whom she was closely associated. The assistant to whom she repeatedly refers as "Miss G." appears from her letters to have been Kate Ball. Her vagueness as to her own position and the status of the various surgeons with whom she came in contact may have been consciously contrived to prevent specific identification of certain individuals of whom she was sharply critical. No explanation can be offered for the several statements in the book which convey the impression that her hospital service began in 1861. Records in the National Archives show that she assumed her duties at Chimborazo on December 18, 1862, and no evidence was found of prior connection with any other hospital.

A Southern Woman's Story was first published in 1879 by G. W. Carleton of New York and S. Low of London. The number of copies published is not known. It was probably small, as very few of the books have been offered for sale during recent years.

In preparing the memoir for re-issue I have broken up some long paragraphs, divided the narrative into chapters and provided chapter headings. Arrangement into chapters and the adding of an index made it possible to delete the topical listings which comprise the four pages of "contents" in the prior edition. I have added the name of Mrs. George W. Randolph who was referred to simply as "the wife of the then acting Secretary of War," to identify definitely the person responsible for Mrs. Pember's appointment as matron at Chimborazo. In a few instances I have spelled out the names of persons for whom Mrs. Pember gave only initials. In her personal copy of *A Southern Woman's Story,* now in the possession of her grand-nieces, Phoebe wrote six minor corrections; these have been included in the revision. No changes have been made that would alter meaning.

＊   ＊   ＊   ＊   ＊   ＊

In searching for material that might be useful in preparing a new edition of *A Southern Woman's Story,* it was my good fortune to find nine manuscript letters written by Phoebe during the Civil War. Seven of these letters are in the Phoebe Pember and Phillips-Myers Collections at the University of North Carolina and two of them (25 June and 13 September 1863) are in the Philip Phillips Papers at the Library of Congress. Since these letters had not been published, and since they contain much new and valuable material, not only about Phoebe and her hospital experiences, but also about life in Confederate Richmond, it was decided to combine them with the text of *A Southern Woman's Story* to make a new book of two parts. It was also deemed advisable to add a sub-title so as to make the caption more precisely descriptive of the content of the book.

In addition to those already mentioned, the sources most useful in preparing this work were: Manuscript Records of Chimborazo Hospital in the National Archives; *Medical and Surgical History of the War of the Rebellion* (6 vols., Washington, 1870-1888); W. B. Blanton, *Medicine in Virginia in the Nineteenth Century* (Richmond, 1933); H. H. Cunningham, *Doctors in Gray: The Confederate Medical Service* (Baton Rouge, 1958); Mary Boykin Chesnut, *A Diary from Dixie* (Boston, 1949); Mrs. Burton Harrison, *Recollections Grave and Gay* (New York, 1911); and T. C. DeLeon, *Belles, Beaux and Brains of the 60's* (New York, 1907). A careful search of Savannah and Pittsburgh newspapers failed to turn up an obituary of Mrs. Pember, but a brief announcement of her funeral was found in the March 6, 1913 issue of the Savannah *Morning News* in the Library of Congress

Pictures of Mrs. Pember, and considerable information about her life and background, were generously provided by her grand-nieces—granddaughters of Mrs. Philip Phillips—Misses Fanny, Georgina and Daisy Phillips—whose attractive home in Savannah it was my pleasure to visit. I am also indebted to Mrs. Lilla Hawes, capable and cooperative Director of the Georgia Historical Society at Savannah for hospitality and for valuable assistance in locating materials.

For generous help in obtaining illustrations, I wish to thank the following persons: William M. E. Rachal, and John Melville Jennings of the Virginia Historical Society; W. Edwin Hemphill, Editor of *Virginia Cavalcade;* William F. Tompkins, Comptroller, Medical College of Virginia; Mrs. Ralph Catterall, Curator of Prints and Manuscripts, the Valentine Museum; Miss India Thomas and Miss Eleanor S. Brockenbrough, the Confederate

Museum; William J. Van Schreeven, Virginia State Archivist; Mrs. Hermon Winfrey and Mr. Robert F. Williams, Richmond, Virginia; Hirst Milhollen, Library of Congress; Miss Josephine Cobb, National Archives; and Miss Sheilah Parker, National Library of Medicine.

To Victor Gondos, Jr., Robert Land, J. W. Patton, Mary Givens Bryan and their associates, respectively, in the National Archives, the Library of Congress, the Southern Historical Collection of the University of North Carolina and the Georgia Department of Archives and History, I am deeply grateful for help in obtaining facsimiles of Pember materials.

My greatest debt, in the preparation of this book as well as its predecessors in the series, is to my collaborator and good friend, Seale Johnson, amiable and efficient Director of the McCowat-Mercer Press, whose assistance consistently goes far beyond that normally given by a publisher and who seems always to be more interested in turning out a quality product than in realizing a handsome profit.

BELL IRVIN WILEY

Emory University

A
Southern Woman's
Story

CHAPTER 1

ENTRY INTO MAN'S DOMAIN

SOON AFTER the breaking out of the Southern war, the need of hospitals, properly organized and arranged, began to be felt, and buildings adapted for the purpose were secured by government. Richmond, being nearest the scene of action, took the lead in this matter, and the formerly hastily contrived accommodations for the sick were soon replaced by larger, more comfortable and better ventilated buildings.

The expense of keeping up small hospitals had forced itself upon the attention of the Surgeon General, Samuel P. Moore, who on that account gradually incorporated them into half-a-dozen immense establishments, strewn around the suburbs. These were called Camp Jackson, Camp Winder, Chimborazo Hospital, Stuart Hospital and Howard Grove; and were arranged so that from thirty to forty wards formed a division, and generally five divisions a hospital. Each ward accommodated from thirty to forty patients, according to the immediate need for space. Besides the sick wards, similar buildings were used for official purposes, for in these immense establishments every necessary trade was carried on. There were the carpenter's, blacksmith's, apothecary's and shoemaker's shops; the ice-houses, commissary's and quartermaster's departments; and offices for surgeons, stewards, baggage-masters and clerks. Each division was furnished with all these, and each hospital presented to the eye the appearance of a small village.

There was no reason why, with this preparation for the wounded and sick, that they should not have received all the benefit of good nursing and food; but soon rumors began to circulate that there was something wrong in hospital administration, and Congress, desirous of remedying omissions, passed a law by which matrons were appointed. They had no official recognition, ranking even below stewards from a military point of view. Their pay was almost nominal from the depreciated nature of the currency. There had been a great deal of desultory visiting and nursing, by the women, previous to this law taking effect, resulting in more harm than benefit to the patients; and now that the field was open, a few, very few ladies, and a great many inefficient and uneducated women, hardly above the laboring classes, applied for and filled the offices.

The women of the South had been openly and violently rebellious from the moment they thought their states' rights touched. They incited the men to struggle in support of their views, and whether right or wrong, sustained them nobly to the end. They were the first to rebel—the last to succumb. Taking an active part in all that came within their sphere, and often compelled to go beyond this when the field demanded as many soldiers as could be raised; feeling a passion of interest in every man in the gray uniform of the Confederate service; they were doubly anxious to give comfort and assistance to the sick and wounded. In the course of a long and harassing war, with ports blockaded and harvests burnt, rail tracks constantly torn up, so that supplies of food were cut off, and sold always at exorbitant prices, no appeal was ever made to the women of the South, individually or collectively, that did not meet with a ready response. There was no parade of generosity; no published lists of donations, inspected by public eyes. What was contributed was given unostentatiously, whether a barrel of coffee or the only half bottle of wine in the giver's possession.

About this time one of these large hospitals was to be opened, and the wife of George W. Randolph, Secretary of War, offered me the superintendence—rather a startling proposition to a woman used to all the comforts of luxurious life. Foremost among the Virginia women, she had given her resources of mind and means to the sick, and her graphic and earnest representations of the benefit a good and determined woman's rule could effect in such a position settled the result in my mind. The natural idea that such a life would be injurious to the delicacy and refinement of a lady—that her nature would become deteriorated and her sensibilities blunted, was rather appalling. But the first step only costs, and that was soon taken.

A preliminary interview with the surgeon-in-chief gave necessary confidence. He was energetic—capable—skillful. A man with ready oil to pour upon troubled waters. Difficulties melted away beneath the warmth of his ready interest, and mountains sank into mole-hills when his quick comprehension had surmounted and leveled them. However troublesome daily increasing annoyances became, if they could not be removed, his few and ready words sent applicants and grumblers home satisfied to do the best they could. Wisely he decided to have an educated and efficient woman at the head of his hospital, and having succeeded, never allowed himself to forget that fact.

The day after my decision was made found me at "headquarters," the only two-story building on hospital ground, then occupied by the chief surgeon and his clerks. He had not yet made his appearance that morning, and while awaiting him, many of his corps, who had expected in horror the advent of female supervision, walked in and out, evidently inspecting me. There was at that time a general ignorance on all sides, except among the hospital officials, of the decided objection on the part of the latter to the carrying out of a law which they prognosticated would entail "petticoat government;" but there was no mistaking the stage-whisper which reached my ears from the open door of the office that morning, as the little contract surgeon passed out and informed a friend he met, in a tone of ill-concealed disgust, that *"one of them had come."*

CHAPTER 2

FIRST DAYS AT CHIMBORAZO HOSPITAL

To THOSE not acquainted with hospital arrangements, some explanations are necessary. To each hospital is assigned a surgeon-in-chief. To each *division* of the hospital, a surgeon in charge. To each *ward* of the division, an assistant surgeon. But when the press of business is great, contract doctors are also put in charge of wards. The surgeon-in-chief makes an inspection each day, calling a board of inferior surgeons to make their report to him. The surgeon in charge is always on the ground, goes through the wards daily, consulting with his assistants and reforming abuses, making his report daily to the surgeon-in-chief. The assistant surgeon has only his one or two wards to attend, passing through them twice each day and prescribing. In cases of danger he calls in the surgeon in charge for advice or assistance. The contract surgeons performed the same duties as assistant surgeons, but ranked below them, as they were not commissioned officers and received less pay.

Each ward had its corps of nurses, unfortunately not practised or expert in their duties, as they had been sick or wounded men, convalescing and placed in that position, —however ignorant they might be,—till strong enough for field duty. This arrangement bore very hard upon all interested, and harder upon the sick, as it entailed constant supervision and endless teaching; but the demand

for men in the field was too imperative to allow those who
were fit for their duties there to be detained for nursing
purposes, however skillful they may have become.

Besides these mentioned, the hospital contained an endless horde of stewards and their clerks; surgeons' clerks;
commissaries and their clerks; quartermasters and clerks;
apothecaries and clerks; baggage-masters; forage-masters;
wagon-masters; cooks; bakers; carpenters; shoemakers;
ward-inspectors; ambulance-drivers; and many more;
forgotten hangers-on, to whom the soldiers gave the name
of "hospital rats" in common with would-be invalids who
resisted being cured from a disinclination to field service.
They were so called, it is to be supposed, from the difficulty of getting rid of either species. Still, many of them
were physically unfit for the field.

Among these conflicting elements, all belittled at a time
of general enthusiasm by long absence from the ennobling
influences of military service, and all striving with rare
exceptions to gain the small benefits and few comforts so
scarce in the Confederacy, I was introduced that day by
the surgeon in charge. He was a cultivated, gentlemanly
man, kind-hearted when he remembered to be so, and
very much afraid of any responsibility resting upon his
shoulders. No preparations had been made by him for his
female department. He escorted me into a long, low,
whitewashed building, open from end to end, called for
two benches, and then, with entire composure, as if surrounding circumstances were most favorable, commenced
an æsthetic conversation on *belles lettres,* female influence,
and the first, last and only novel published during the
war. (It was a translation of *Joseph the Second,* printed
on gray and bound in marbled wall-paper.) A neat compliment offered at leave-taking rounded off the interview,
with a parting promise from him to send me the carpen-

ter to make partitions and shelves for office, parlor, laundry, pantry and kitchen. The steward was then summoned for consultation, and my representative reign began.

A stove was unearthed; very small, very rusty, and fit only for a family of six. There were then about six hundred men upon the matron's diet list, the illest ones to be supplied with food from my kitchen, and the convalescents from the steward's, called, in contra-distinction from mine, "the big kitchen." Just then my mind could hardly grope through the darkness that clouded it, as to what were my special duties, but one mental spectrum always presented itself—*chicken soup.*

Having vaguely heard of requisitions, I then and there made my first, in very unofficial style. A polite request sent through "Jim" (a small black boy) to the steward for a pair of chickens. They came instantly ready dressed for cooking. Jim picked up some shavings, kindled up the stove, begged, borrowed or stole (either act being lawful to his mind), a large iron pot from the big kitchen. For the first time I cut up with averted eyes a raw bird, and the Rubicon was passed.

My readers must not suppose that this picture applies generally to all our hospitals, or that means and appliances so early in the war for food and comfort, were so meagre. This state of affairs was only the result of accident and some misunderstanding. The surgeon of my hospital naturally thought I had informed myself of the power vested in me by virtue of my position, and, having some experience, would use the rights given me by the law passed in Congress, to arrange my own department; and I, on reading the bill, could only understand that the office was one that dovetailed the duties of housekeeper and cook, nothing more.

In the meantime the soup was boiling, and was undeniably a success, from the perfume it exhaled. Nature may not have intended me for a Florence Nightingale, but a kitchen proved my worth. Frying-pans, griddles, stewpans and coffee-pots soon became my household gods. The niches must have been prepared years previously, invisible to the naked eye but still there.

Gaining courage from familiarity with my position, a venture across the lane brought me to the nearest ward (they were all separate buildings, it must be remembered, covering a half mile of ground in a circle, one story high, with long, low windows opening back in a groove against the inside wall), and, under the first I peeped in, lay the shadow of a man extended on his bed, pale and attennuated.

What woman's heart would not melt and make itself a home where so much needed?

His wants were inquired into, and, like all the humbler class of men, who think that unless they have been living on hog and hominy they are starved, he complained of not having eaten anything "for three mortal weeks."

In the present state of the kitchen larder, there was certainly not much of a choice, and I was as yet ignorant of the capabilities of the steward's department. However, soup was suggested, as a great soother of "misery in his back," and a generous supply of adjectives prefixed for flavor—"nice, hot, good chicken soup." The suggestion was received kindly. If it was very nice he would take some: "he was never, though, much of a hand for drinks." My mind rejected the application of words, but matter not mind, was the subject under consideration.

All my gastronomic experience revolted against soup without the sick man's parsley; and Jim, my acting partner, volunteered to get some at a mysterious place he always called "The Dutchman's," so at last, armed with a bowl full of the decoction, duly salted, peppered, and seasoned, I again sought my first patient.

He rose deliberately—so deliberately that I felt sensible of the great favor he was conferring. He smoothed his tangled locks with a weak hand, took a piece of well-masticated tobacco from between three or four solitary teeth, but still the soup was unappropriated, and it appeared evident that some other preliminaries were to be arranged. The novelty of my position, added to a lively imagination, suggested fears that he might think it necessary to arise for compliment sake; and hospital clothing being made to suit the scarcity and expense of homespun, the idea was startling. But my suspense did not continue long; he was only seeking for a brown-covered tract hid under his pillow.

Did he intend to read grace before meat? No, he simply wanted a pocket-handkerchief, which cruel war had denied; so without comment a leaf was quietly abstracted and used for that purpose. The result was satisfactory, for the next moment the bowl was taken from my hand, and the first spoonful of soup transmitted to his mouth.

It was an awful minute! My fate seemed to hang upon the fiat of that uneducated palate. A long painful gulp, a "judgmatical" shake of the head, *not* in the affirmative, and the bowl traveled slowly back to my extended hand.

"My mammy's soup was not like that," he whined. "But I might worry a little down if it war'n't for them *weeds* a-floating round."

Well! why be depressed? There may not after all be any actual difference between weeds and herbs.

CHAPTER 3

FIRST SKIRMISH FOR THE WHISKEY BARREL

AFTER that first day improvements rapidly progressed. Better stoves, and plenty of them, were put up; closets enclosed; china or its substitutes, pottery and tin, supplied. I learned to make requisitions and to use my power. The coffee, tea, milk, and all other luxuries provided for the sick wards, were, through my demand, turned over to me; also a co-laborer with Jim, that young gentleman's disposition proving to be like my old horse, who pulled well and steadily in single harness, but when tried in double team, left all the hard work to the last comer. However, honor to whom honor is due. He gave me many hints which my higher intelligence had overlooked, comprehended by him more through instinct than reason, and was as clever at gathering trophies for my kitchen as General Benjamin F. Butler was—for other purposes.

Still my office did not rise above that of chief cook, for I dared not leave my kitchen unattended for a moment, till Doctor James B. McCaw, one day, passing the window, and seeing me seated on a low bench peeling potatoes, appeared much surprised, and inquired where my cooks were. Explanations followed, a copy of hospital rules was sent for, and authority found to provide the matron's department with suitable attendants. A gentle, sweet-tempered lady, extremely neat and efficient, was appointed assistant matron, also three or four cooks and bakers. Jim and his companion were degraded into drawers of water and hewers of wood; that is to say, these ought to have been their duties, but their occupation became walking gentlemen. On assuming their out-door labors, their allegiance to me ceased, and the trophies which formerly swelled my list of dainties for the sick were nightly carried "down the hill," where everything that was missed disappeared.

Then began the routine of hospital life in regular order. Breakfast at seven in the morning in summer and eight in winter. Coffee, tea, milk, bread of various kinds, and butter or molasses, and whatever meats could be saved from the yesterday's dinner. This was in the first year of the war. Afterwards we were not able to be so luxurious. The quantity supplied would be impartially divided among the wards with the retention of the delicacies for the very ill men.

The ward-masters with their nurses gathered three times a day, for each meal, around my office window adjoining the kitchen, with large wooden trays and piles of plates, waiting to receive the food, each being helped in turn to a fair division. If an invalid craved any particular dish the nurse mentioned the want, and if not contrary to the surgeon's order, it, or its nearest approximation was allowed him.

After breakfast the assistant surgeons visited their respective wards, making out their diet lists, or rather filling them up, for the forms were printed, and only the invalid's name, number of his bed, and his diet—light, half, or full, were required to be specified, also the quantity of whiskey desired for each. Dinner and supper served in the same way, except for the very sick. They had what they desired, in or out of season, and all seemed to object to the nutriment concocted from those tasteless and starchy compounds of wheat, corn and arrowroot, that are so thick and heavy to swallow, and so little nutritious. They were served hot from the fire, or congealed from the ice (for after the suffering caused from the deprivation of ice the first summer of the war was felt, each hospital built its own ice-house, which was well filled by the next season).

At two o'clock the regular dinner of poultry, beef, ham, fish and vegetables, was distributed. (After the first year our bill of fare decreased much in variety.) Supper at six. The chief matron sat at her table, the diet lists arranged before her, each day, and managed so that no especial ward should invariably be the first served, although they were named in alphabetical order. Any necessary instructions of the surgeons were noted and attended to, sometimes accompanied with observations of her own, not always complimentary to those gentlemen, nor prudent as regarded herself.

The orders ran somewhat in this fashion: "Chicken soup for twenty—beef tea for forty—tea and toast for fifty." A certain Mr. Jones had expressed his abhorrence of tea and toast, so I asked the nurse why he gave it to him.

He answered that the diet was ordered by the surgeon, but Jones said he would not touch it, for he never ate slops, and so he had eaten nothing for two days.

"Well, what does he wish?"

"The doctor says tea and toast" (reiterating his first remark).

"Did you tell the doctor he would not eat it?"

"*I* told the doctor, and *he* told the doctor."

"Perhaps he did not hear, or understand you."

"Yes, he did. He only said that he wanted that man particularly to have tea and toast, though I told him Jones threw it up regularly; so he put it down again, and said Jones was out of his head, and Jones says the doctor is a fool."

My remark upon this was that Jones could not be so very much out of his head—an observation that entailed subsequent consequences. The habit so common among physicians when dealing with uneducated people, of insisting upon particular kinds of diet, irrespective of the patient's tastes, was a peculiar grievance that no complaint during four years ever remedied.

Although visiting my wards in the morning for the purpose of speaking words of comfort to the sick, and remedying any apparent evils which had been overlooked or forgotten by the surgeons when going their rounds, the fear that the nourishment furnished had not suited the tastes of men debilitated to an extreme not only by disease and wounds, but also by the privations and exposures of camp life, would again take me among them in the afternoon. Then would come heart-sickness and discouragement, for out of a hundred invalids, seventy, on an average, would assert that they had not taken any nourishment whatever. This was partly owing to habit or imitation of others, and partly to the human desire to enlist sympathy.

The common soldier has a horror of a hospital, and with the rejection of food comes the hope that weakness will increase proportionally, and a furlough become necessary. Besides, the human palate, to relish good food, must be as well educated as other organs for other purposes. Who appreciates a good painting until his eye is trained, or fine harmony until the ear is cultivated? And why should not the same rule apply to tongue and taste? Men who never before had been sick, or swallowed those starchy, flavorless compounds young surgeons are so fond of prescribing, repudiated them invariably, in spite of my skill in making them palatable. They were suspicious of the *terra incognita* from which they sprang, having had no experience heretofore, and suspicion always engenders disgust.

Daily inspection too, convinced me that great evils still existed under my rule, in spite of my zealous care for my patients. For example, the monthly barrel of whiskey which I was entitled to draw still remained at the dispensary under the guardianship of the apothecary and his clerks, and quarts and pints were issued through any order coming from surgeons or their substitutes, so that the contents were apt to be gone long before I was entitled to draw more, and my sick would suffer for want of the stimulant. There were many suspicious circumstances connected with this *institution;* for the monthly barrel was an institution and a very important one. Indeed, if it is necessary to have a hero for this matter-of-fact narrative, the whiskey barrel will have to step forward and make his bow.

So again I referred to the hospital bill passed by Congress, which provided that liquors in common with other luxuries, belonged to the matron's department, and in an evil moment, such an impulse as tempted Pandora to open the fatal casket assailed me, and I despatched the bill, flanked by a formal requisition for the liquor. An answer came in the shape of the head surgeon. He declared I would find "the charge most onerous," that "whiskey was required at all hours, sometimes in the middle of the night, and even if I remained at the hospital, he would not like me to be disturbed," "it was constantly needed for medicinal purposes," "he was responsible for its proper application;" but I was not convinced, and withstood all argument and persuasion. He was proverbially sober himself, but I was aware why both commissioned and non-commissioned officers opposed violently the removal of the liquor to my quarters. So, the printed law being at hand for reference, I nailed my colors to the mast, and that evening all the liquor was in my pantry and the key in my pocket.

CHAPTER 4

"ARE YOU MARRIED?"

THE FIRST RESTRAINTS of a woman's presence had now worn away, and the thousand miseries of my position began to make themselves felt. The young surgeons (not all gentlemen, although their profession should have made them aspirants to the character), and the nurses played into each other's hands. If the former were off on a frolic, the latter would conceal the absence of necessary attendance by erasing the date of the diet list of the day before and substituting the proper one, duplicating the prescription also, and thus preventing inquiry. In like manner the assistant surgeons, to whom the nurses were alone responsible, would give them leave of absence, concealing the fact from the head surgeon, which could easily be effected; then the patients would suffer, and complaints from the matron be obnoxious and troublesome, and also entirely out of her line of business. She was to be cook and housekeeper, and nothing more.

Added now to other difficulties was the dragonship of the Hesperides,—the guarding of the liquefied golden fruit to which access had been open to a certain extent before her reign,—and for many, many months the petty persecutions endured from all the small fry around almost exceeded human patience to bear. What the surgeon in charge could do to mitigate the annoyances entailed he conscientiously did; but with the weight of a large hospital on his not very strong mind, and very little authority delegated to him, he could hardly reform abuses or punish silly attacks, so small in the abstract, so great in the aggregate.

The eventful evening when Mr. Jones revolted against tea and toast, my unfortunate remark intended for no particular ear but caught by the nurse, that the patient's intellects could not be confused if he called his surgeon a fool, brought forth a recriminating note to me. It was from that maligned and incensed gentleman, and proved the progenitor of a long series of communications of the same character; a family likeness pervading them all. They generally commenced with "Dr. —— presents his compliments to the chief matron," continuing with "Mrs. —— and I," and ending with "you and him." They were difficult to understand and more difficult to endure. Accustomed to be treated with extreme deference and courtesy by the highest officials connected with the goverment, moving in the same social grade I had always occupied when beyond hospital bounds, the change was appalling.

The inundation of notes that followed for many months could not have been sent back unopened, the last refuge under the circumstances, for some of them might have related to the well-being of the sick. My pen certainly was ready enough, but could I waste my thunderbolts in such an atmosphere?

The depreciated currency, which purchased only at fabulous prices by this time; the poor pay the government (feeling the necessity of keeping up the credit of its paper) gave to its officials; the natural craving for luxuries that had been but common food before the war, caused appeals to be made to me, sometimes for the applicant, oftener for his sick wife or child, so constantly, that had I given even one-tenth of the gifts demanded there would have been but little left for my patients.

It was hard to refuse, for the plea that it was not mine but merely a charge confided to me, was looked upon as a pretext; outsiders calculating upon the quantity issued to my department and losing sight of the ownership of that quantity.

Half a dozen convalescent men would lose their taste-less dinner daily at the steward's table, and beg for "any-thing" which would mean turkey and oysters. Others "had been up all night and craved a cup of coffee and a roll," and as for diseases among commissioned and non-com-missioned men, caused by entire destitution of whiskey, and only to be cured by it—their name was legion. Every pound of coffee, every ounce of whiskey, bushel of flour or vegetables duly weighed before delivery, was intended for its particular consumers; who, if they even could not eat or drink what was issued for them watched their prop-erty zealously, and claimed it too. So what had I to give away?

The necessity of refusing the live-long day, forced upon naturally generous tempers, makes them captious and uncivil, and under the pressure the soft answer cannot be evoked to turn away wrath. Demands would increase until they amounted to persecutions when the refusals became the rule instead of the exception, and the breach thus made grew wider day by day, until "my hand was against every man, and every man's hand against me."

Besides, there was little gratitude felt in a hospital, and certainly none expressed. The mass of patients were uneducated men, who had lived by the sweat of their brow, and gratitude is an exotic plant, reared in a refined atmosphere, kept free from coarse contact and nourished by unselfishness. Common natures look only with surprise at great sacrifices and cunningly avail themselves of the benefits they bestow, but give nothing in return,—not even the satisfaction of allowing the giver to feel that the care bestowed has been beneficial; *that* might entail compensation of some kind, and in their ignorance they fear the nature of the equivalent which might be demanded.

Still, pleasant episodes often occurred to vary disappointments and lighten duties.

"Kin you writ me a letter?" drawled a whining voice from a bed in one of the wards, a cold day in '62.

The speaker was an up-country Georgian, one of the kind called "Goubers" by the soldiers generally; lean, yellow, attennuated, with wispy strands of hair hanging over his high, thin cheek bones. He put out a hand to detain me and the nails were like claws.

"Why do you not let the nurse cut your nails?"

"Because I aren't got any spoon, and I use them instead."

"Will you let me have your hair cut then? You can't get well with all that dirty hair hanging about your eyes and ears."

"No, I can't git my hair cut, kase as how I promised my mammy that I would let it grow till the war be over. Oh, it's onlucky to cut it!"

"Then I can't write any letter for you. Do what I wish you to do, and then I will oblige you."

This was plain talking. The hair was cut (I left the nails for another day), my portfolio brought, and sitting by the side of his bed I waited for further orders. They came with a formal introduction,—"for Mrs. Marthy Brown."

"My dear Mammy:

"I hope this finds you well, as it leaves me well, and I
hope that I shall git a furlough Christmas, and come and
see you, and I hope that you will keep well, and all the
folks be well by that time, as I hopes to be well myself.
This leaves me in good health, as I hope it finds you
and——"

But here I paused, as his mind seemed to be going
round in a circle, and asked him a few questions about his
home, his position during the last summer's campaign,
how he got sick, and where his brigade was at that time.
Thus furnished with some material to work upon, the
letter proceeded rapidly. Four sides were conscientiously
filled, for no soldier would think a letter worth sending
home that showed any blank paper.

Transcribing his name, the number of his ward and
proper address, so that an answer might reach him—the
composition was read to him. Gradually his pale face
brightened, a sitting posture was assumed with difficulty
(for, in spite of his determined effort in his letter "to be
well," he was far from convalescence). As I folded and
directed it, contributed the expected five-cent stamp, and
handed it to him, he gazed cautiously around to be sure
there were no listeners.

"Did you writ all that?" he asked, whispering, but with
great emphasis.

"Yes."

"Did *I* say all that?"

"I think you did."

A long pause of undoubted admiration—astonishment
ensued. What was working in that poor mind? Could it
be that Psyche had stirred one of the delicate plumes of
her wing and touched that dormant soul?

"Are you married?" the harsh voice dropped very low.

"I am not. At least, I am a widow."

He rose still higher in bed. He pushed away desperately the tangled hay on his brow. A faint color fluttered over the hollow cheek, and stretching out a long piece of bone with a talon attached, he gently touched my arm and with constrained voice whispered mysteriously:

"You wait!"

And readers, I *am* waiting still; and I here caution the male portion of creation who may adore through their mental powers, to respect my confidence, and not seek to shake my constancy.

Other compliments were paid me, perhaps not of so conclusive a nature, and they were noticeable from their originality and novelty, but they were also rare. Expression was not a gift among the common soldiers. "You will wear them little feet away," said a rough Kentuckian, "running around so much. They ar'n't much to boast of anyway." Was not this as complimentary as the lover who compared his mistress's foot to a dream; and much more comprehensible?

At intervals the lower wards, unused except in times of great need, for they were unfurnished with any comforts, would be filled with rough soldiers from camp, sent to recuperate after field service, who may not have seen a female face for months; and though generally too much occupied to notice them, their partly concealed, but determined regard would become embarrassing.

One day, while directing arrangements with a ward-master, my attention was attracted by the pertinacious staring of a rough-looking Texan. He walked round and round me in rapidly narrowing circles, examining every detail of my dress, face, and figure; his eye never fixing upon any particular part for a moment but traveling incessantly all over me. It seemed the wonder of the mind at the sight of a new creation. I moved my position; he shifted his to suit the new arrangement—again a change was made, so obviously to get out of his range of vision, that with a delicacy of feeling that the roughest men always treated me with, he desisted from his inspection so far, that though his person made no movement, his neck twisted round to accommodate his eyes, till I supposed some progenitor of his family had been an owl. The men began to titter, and my patience became exhausted.

"What is the matter, my man? Did you never see a woman before?"

"Jerusalem!" he ejaculated, not making the slightest motion towards withdrawing his determined notice, "I never did see such a nice one. Why, you's as pretty as a pair of red shoes with green strings."

These were the two compliments laid upon the shrine of my vanity during four years' contact with thousands of patients, and I commit them to paper to stand as a visionary portrait, to prove to my readers that a woman with attractions similar to a pair of red shoes with green strings must have some claim to be the apple of Paris.

CHAPTER 5

A DISAPPOINTING EXPERIMENT

SCENES of pathos occurred daily—scenes that wrung the heart and forced the dew of pity from the eyes; but feeling that enervated the mind and relaxed the body was a sentimental luxury that was not to be indulged in. There was too much work to be done, too much active exertion required, to allow the mental or physical powers to succumb. They were severely taxed each day. Perhaps they balanced, and so kept each other from sinking. There was, indeed, but little leisure to sentimentalize, the necessity for action being ever present.

After the battle of Fredericksburg, while giving small doses of brandy to a dying man, a low, pleasant voice, said "Madam." It came from a youth not over eighteen years of age, seeming very ill, but so placid, with that earnest, far-away gaze, so common to the eyes of those who are looking their last on this world. Does God in his mercy give a glimpse of coming peace, past understanding, that we see reflected in the dying eyes into which we look with such strong yearning to fathom what they see? He shook his head in negative to all offers of food or drink or suggestions of softer pillows and lighter covering.

"I want Perry," was his only wish.

On inquiry I found that Perry was the friend and companion who marched by his side in the field and slept next to him in camp, but of whose whereabouts I was ignorant. Armed with a requisition from our surgeon, I sought him among the sick and wounded at all the other hospitals. I found him at Camp Jackson, put him in my ambulance, and on arrival at my own hospital found my patient had dropped asleep. A bed was brought and placed at his side, and Perry, only slightly wounded, laid upon it. Just then the sick boy awoke wearily, turned over, and the half-unconscious eye fixed itself. He must have been dreaming of the meeting, for he still distrusted the reality. Illness had spiritualized the youthful face; the transparent forehead, the delicate brow so clearly defined, belonged more to heaven than earth. As he recognized his comrade the wan and expressionless lips curved into the happiest smile—the angel of death had brought the light of summer skies to that pale face. "Perry," he cried, "Perry," and not another word, but with one last effort he threw himself into his friend's arms, the radiant eyes closed, but the smile still remained—he was dead.

There was but little sensibility exhibited by soldiers for the fate of their comrades in field or hospital. The results of war are here today and gone tomorrow. I stood still, spell-bound by that youthful death-bed, when my painful revery was broken upon by a drawling voice from a neighboring bed, which had been calling me by such peculiar names or titles that I had been oblivious to whom they were addressed.

"Look here. I say, Aunty!—Mammy!—You!" Then, in despair, "Missus! Mauma! Kin you gim me sich a thing as a b'iled sweet pur-r-rta-a-a-tu-ur? I b'long to the Twenty-secun' Nor' Ka-a-a-li-i-na rigiment." I told the nurse to remove his bed from proximity to his dead neighbor, thinking that in the low state of his health from fever the sight might affect his nerves, but he treated the suggestion with contempt.

"Don't make no sort of difference to *me;* they dies all around *me* in the field—don't trouble *me.*"

The wounded men at this time began to make serious complaints that the liquor issued did **not** reach them, and no vigilance on my part appeared to check the improper appropriation of it, or lead to any discovery of the thieves in the wards. There were many obstacles to be surmounted before proper precautions could be taken. Lumber was so expensive that closets in each ward were out of the question, and if made locks could not be purchased for any amount of money. The liquor therefore, when it left my quarters, was open to any passer-by in the wards who would watch his opportunity; so, although I had strong and good reasons for excluding female nurses, the supposition that liquor would be no temptation to them, and would be more apt to reach its proper destination through their care, determined me to engage them.

Unlucky thought, born in an evil hour!

There was no lack of applications when the want was circulated, but my choice hesitated between ladies of education and position, who I knew would be willing to aid me, and the common class of respectable servants. The latter suited best, because it was to be supposed they would be more amenable to authority. They were engaged, and the very sick wards divided among three of them. They were to keep the bed-clothing in order, receive and dispense the liquor, carry any delicacy in the way of food where it was most needed, and in fact do anything reasonable that was requested. The last stipulation was dwelt upon strongly.

The next day my new corps were in attendance, and the different liquors, beverages and stimulants delivered to them under the black looks of the ward-masters. No. 1

received hers silently. She was a cross-looking woman from North Carolina, painfully ugly, or rather what is termed hard-featured, and apparently very taciturn; the last quality rather an advantage. She had hardly left my kitchen when she returned with all the drinks, and a very indignant face.

In reply to inquiries made she proved her taciturnity was not chronic. She asserted loudly that she was a decent woman, and "was not going anywhere in a place where a man sat up on his bed in his shirt, and the rest laughed— she knew they were laughing at her." The good old proverb that talking is silver but silence is gold had impressed itself on my mind long before this, so I silently took her charge from her, telling her that a hospital was no place for a person of her delicate sensibilities, and at the same time holding up Miss G. and myself (who were young enough to be her daughters), as examples for her imitation.

She answered truly that we acted as we pleased and so would she; and that was the last I saw of her. What her ideas of hospital life were I never inquired, and shall never know.

No. 2 came briskly forward. She was a plausible, light-haired, light-eyed and light-complexioned Englishwoman; very petite, with a high nose. She had come to the hospital with seven trunks, which ought to have been a warning to me, but she brought such strong recommendations from responsible parties that they warped my judgment. She received the last trust handed her—an open pitcher of hot punch—with averted head, nose turned aside, and held it at arm's length with a high disdain mounted upon her high nose. Her excuse for this antipathy was that the smell of liquor was "awful," she "could not a-bear it," and "it turned her witals." This was rather suspicious, but we deferred judgment.

Dinner was distributed. No. 2 appeared, composed, vigilant and attentive to her duties, carrying her delicacies of food to her wards with the assistance of the nurses. No. 3, an inoffensive woman did the same, and all worked well. That afternoon, when I had retired to my little sanctum to take the one hour's rest that I allowed myself each day undisturbed, Miss G. put her head in the door with an apprehensive look and said, "the new matrons wished to see me." They were admitted, and my high-nosed friend, who had been elected spokeswoman it seems, said after a few preliminaries, with a toss of her head and a couple of sniffs that I "seemed to have made myself very comfortable."

This was assented to graciously. She added that other people were not, who were quite as much entitled to *style*. This also remained undisputed, and then she stated her real grievance, that they "were not satisfied, for I had not invited them to call upon me, or into my room," and "they considered themselves quite as much ladies as I was." I answered I was glad to hear it, and hoped they would always act as ladies should, and in a way suitable to the title. There was an evident desire on her part to say more, but she had not calculated upon the style of reception, and therefore was thrown out beyond her line of action, so she civilly requested me to call and inspect their quarters that they were dissatisfied with. An hour later I did so, and found them sitting around a sociable spittoon, with a friendly box of snuff—dipping! I found it impossible to persuade them that the government was alone responsible for their poor quarters, they persisted in holding me answerable.

The next day, walking through one of the wards under No. 2's charge, I found a part of the building, of about eight to ten feet square, portioned off, a roughly improvised plank partition dividing this temporary room from the rest of the ward. Seated comfortably therein was the new matron, entrenched among her trunks. A neat table and comfortable chair, abstracted from my few kitchen appurtenances, added to her comforts. Choice pieces of crockery, remnants of more luxurious times, that had at one time adorned my shelves, were disposed tastefully around, and the drinks issued by me for the patients were conveniently placed at her elbow. She explained that she kept them there to prevent thefts. Perhaps the nausea communicated from their neighborhood had tinted the high nose higher, and there was a defiant look about her, as if she sniffed the battle afar.

It was very near though, and had to be fought, however disagreeable, so I instantly entered into explanations, short, but polite. Each patient being allowed, by law, a certain number of feet, every inch taken therefrom was so much ventilation lost, and the abstraction of as much space as she had taken for illegal purposes was a serious matter, and conflicted with the rules that governed the hospital. Besides this, no woman was allowed to stay in the wards, for obvious reasons.

No. 2, however, was a sensible person, for she did not waste *her* breath in talking; she merely held her position. An appeal made by me to the surgeon of the ward did not result favorably; he said I had engaged her, she belonged to my corps, and was under my supervision: so I sent for the steward.

The steward of a hospital cannot define exactly what his duties are, the difficulty being to find out what they are not. Whenever it has to be decided who has to fill a disagreeable office, the choice invariably falls upon the steward. So a message was sent to his quarters to request him to compel No. 2 to evacuate her hastily improvised premises. He hesitated long, but engaging at last the services of his assistant, a broad-shouldered fighting character, proceeded to eject the new tenant.

He commenced operations by polite explanations; but they were met in a startling manner. She arose and rolled up her sleeves, advancing upon him as he receded down the ward. The sick and wounded men roared with laughter, cheering her on, and she remained mistress of the field. Dinner preparations served as an interlude and silently suppressed, she as usual made her entrée into the kitchen, received the drinks for her ward and vanished. Half an hour elapsed and then the master of the ward in which she had domiciled herself made his report to me, and recounted a pitiful tale.

He was a neat quiet manager, and usually kept his quarters beautifully clean. No. 2, he said, divided the dinner, and whenever she came across a bone in hash or stew, or indeed anything therein displeased her, she took it in her fingers and dashed it upon the floor. With so little to make a hospital gay, this peculiar episode was a god-send to the soldiers, and indeed to all the lookers on. The surgeons stood laughing, in groups, the men crowded to the windows of the belligerent power, and a *coup-d'etat* became necessary.

"Send me the carpenter!" I felt the spirit of Boadicea. The man stepped up; he had always been quiet, civil and obedient.

"Come with me into Ward E."

A few steps took us there.

"Knock down that partition and carry away those boards." It was *un fait accompli.*

But the victory was not gained, only the fortifications stormed and taken, for almost hidden by flying splinters and dust, No. 2 sat among her seven trunks enthroned like Rome among her seven hills.

The story furnishes no further interest, but the result was very annoying. She was put into my ambulance very drunk by this time and sent away, her trunks sent after her. The next day, neatly dressed, she managed to get an interview with the medical director, enlisted his sympathy by a plausible appeal and description of her desolate condition. "A refugee," or "refewgee," as she called herself, "trying to make her living decently," and receiving an order to report at our hospital, was back there by noon. Explanations had to be written, and our surgeon-in-chief to interfere with his authority, before we could get rid of her.

CHAPTER 6

"WHAT COMFORT COULD I GIVE?"

ABOUT THIS TIME (April, 1863),* an attack on Drewry's Bluff, which guarded Richmond on the James River side, was expected, and it was made before the hospital was in readiness to receive the wounded. The cannonading could be heard distinctly in the city, and dense smoke descried rising from the battlefield. The Richmond people had been too often, if not through the wars at least within sight and hearing of its terrors, to feel any great alarm.

The inhabitants lying in groups, crowded the eastern brow of the hill above Rocketts and the James River; overlooking the scene, and discussing the probable results of the struggle; while the change from the dull, full boom of the cannon to the sharp rattle of musketry could be easily distinguished. The sun was setting amidst stormy, purple clouds; and when low upon the horizon sent long slanting rays of yellow light from beneath them, athwart the battle scene, throwing it in strong relief. The shells burst in the air above the fortifications at intervals, and with the aid of glasses dark blue masses of uniforms could be distinguished, though how near the scene of action could not be discerned. About eight o'clock the slightly

---

*Mrs. Pember's memory apparently was faulty as to the time and the engagement. The only two actions of any consequence at Drewry's Bluff occurred in May, 1862 and May, 1864. See *Battles and Leaders of the Civil War*, II, 269-270 and IV, 201-212.

wounded began to straggle in with a bleeding hand, or contused arm or head, bound up in any convenient rag.

Their accounts were meagre, for men in the ranks never know anything about general results—they almost always have the same answer ready, "We druv 'em nowhere."

In another half-hour, vehicles of all kinds crowded in, from a wheelbarrow to a stretcher, and yet no orders had been sent me to prepare for the wounded. Few surgeons had remained in the hospital; the proximity to the field tempting them to join the ambulance committee, or ride to the scene of action; and the officer of the day, left in charge, naturally objected to my receiving a large body of suffering men with no arrangements made for their comfort, and but few in attendance.

I was preparing to leave for my home at the Secretary of the Navy, where I returned every night, when the pitiful sight of the wounded in ambulances, furniture wagons, carts, carriages, and every kind of vehicle that could be impressed detained me. To keep them unattended to, while being driven from one full hospital to another, entailed unnecessary suffering, and the agonized outcry of a desperately wounded man to "take him in, for God's sake, or kill him," decided me to countermand the order of the surgeon in charge that "they must be taken elsewhere, as we had no accommodations prepared." I sent for him, however.

He was a kind-hearted, indolent man, but efficient in his profession, and a gentleman; and seeing my extreme agitation, tried to reason with me, saying our wards were full, except a few vacant and unused ones, which our requisitions had failed to furnish with proper bedding and blankets. Besides, a large number of the surgeons were absent, and the few left would not be able to attend to all the wounds at that late hour of the night. I proposed in reply that the convalescent men should be placed on the floor on blankets, or bed-sacks filled with straw, and the wounded take their place, and, purposely construing his silence into consent, gave the necessary orders, eagerly offering my services to dress simple wounds, and extolling the strength of my nerves.

He let me have my way (may *his* ways be of pleasantness and his paths of peace), and so, giving Miss G. orders to make an unlimited supply of coffee, tea, and stimulants, armed with lint, bandages, castile soap, and a basin of warm water, I made my first essays in the surgical line. I had been spectator often enough to be skillful. The first object that needed my care was an Irishman. He was seated upon a bed with his hands crossed, wounded in both arms by the same bullet. The blood was soon washed away, wet lint applied, and no bones being broken, the bandages easily arranged.

"I hope that I have not hurt you much," I said with some trepidation. "These are the first wounds that I ever dressed."

"Sure they be the most illegant pair of hands that ever touched me, and the lightest," he gallantly answered. "And I am all right now."

From bed to bed till long past midnight, the work continued. Fractured limbs were bathed, washed free from blood and left to the surgeon to set. The men were so exhausted by forced marches, lying in entrenchments and loss of sleep that few even awoke during the operations. If aroused to take nourishment or stimulant they received it with closed eyes, and a speedy relapse into unconsciousness. The next morning, but few had any recollection of the events of the night previous.

There were not as many desperate wounds among the soldiers brought in that night as usual. Strange to say, the ghastliness of wounds varied much in the different battles, perhaps from the nearness or distance of contending parties. One man was an exception and enlisted my warmest sympathy. He was a Marylander although serving in a Virginia company. There was such strength of resignation in his calm blue eye.

"Can you give me a moment?" he said.

"What shall I do for you?"

"Give me some drink to revive me, that I do not die before the surgeon can attend to me."

His pulse was strong but irregular, and telling him that a stimulant might induce fever, and ought only to be administered with a doctor's prescription, I inquired where was he wounded.

Right through the body. Alas!

The doctor's dictum was, "No hope: give him anything he asks for;" but five days and nights I struggled against this decree, fed my patient with my own hands, using freely from the small store of brandy in my pantry and cheering him by words and smiles. The sixth morning on my entrance he turned an anxious eye on my face, the hope had died out of his, for the cold sweat stood in beads there, useless to dry, so constantly were they renewed.

What comfort could I give? Only silently open the Bible, and read to him without comment the ever-living promises of his Maker. Glimpses too of that abode where the "weary are at rest." Tears stole down his cheek, but he was not comforted.

"I am an only son," he said, "and my mother is a widow. Go to her, if you ever get to Baltimore, and tell her that I died in what I consider the defense of civil rights and liberties. I may be wrong. God alone knows. Say how kindly I was nursed, and that I had all I needed. I cannot thank you, for I have no breath, but we will meet up there." He pointed upward and closed his eyes, that never opened again upon this world.

CHAPTER 7

STATE CONSCIOUSNESS AND CONFLICT
IN THE WARDS

E̲ARLIER than this, while hospitals were still partly unorganized, soldiers were brought in from camp or field, and placed in divisions of them, irrespective of rank or state; but soon the officers had more comfortable quarters provided apart from the privates, and separate divisions were also appropriated to men from different sections of the country.

There were so many good reasons for this change that explanations are hardly necessary. Chief among them, was the ease through which, under this arrangement, a man could be found quickly by reference to the books of each particular division. Schedules of where the patients of each state were quartered were published in the daily papers, and besides the materials furnished by government, states and associations, were thus enabled to send satisfactory food and clothing for private distribution. Thus immense contributions, coming weekly from these sources, gave great aid, and enabled us to have a reserved store when government supplies failed.

To those cognizant of these facts, it appeared as if the non-fighting people of the Confederacy had worked as hard and exercised as much self-denial as the soldiers in the field. There was an indescribable pathos lurking at times at the bottom of these heterogeneous home boxes, put up by anxious wives, mothers and sisters; a sad and mute history shadowed forth by the sight of rude, coarse homespun pillow-cases or pocket handkerchiefs, adorned even amid the turmoil of war and poverty of means with an attempt at a little embroidery, or a simple fabrication of lace for trimming. The silent tears dropped over these tokens will never be sung in song or told in story. The little loving expedients to conceal the want of means which each woman resorted to, thinking that if her loved one failed to benefit by the result, other mothers might reap the advantage, is a history in itself.

Piles of sheets, the cotton carded and spun in the one room at home where the family perhaps lived, ate, and slept in the backwoods of Georgia; bales of blankets called so by courtesy, but only the drawing-room carpets, the pride of the heart of thrifty housewives, perhaps their only extravagance in better days, but now cut up for field use. Dozens of pillow slips, not of the coarse product of the home loom, which would be too harsh for the cheek of the invalid, but of the fine bleached cotton of better days, suggesting personal clothing sacrificed to the sick. Boxes of woolen shirts, like Joseph's many-colored coat, created from almost every dressing-gown or flannel skirt in the country.

A thousand evidences of the loving care and energetic labor of the poor, patient ones at home, telling an affecting story that knocked hard at the gates of the heart, were the portals ever so firmly closed; and with all these came letters written by poor ignorant ones who often had no knowledge of how such communications should be addressed.

These letters, making inquiries concerning patients from anxious relatives at home, directed oftener to my office than my name, came in numbers, and were queer mixtures of ignorance, bad grammar, worse spelling and simple feeling. However absurd the style, the love that filled them chastened and purified them. Many are stored away, and though irresistibly ludicrous, are too sacred to print for public amusement.

In them could be detected the prejudices of the different sections. One old lady in upper Georgia wrote a pathetic appeal for a furlough for her son. She called me "My dear sir," while still retaining my feminine address, and though expressing the strongest desire for her son's restoration to health, entreated in moving accents that if his life could not be saved, that he should not be buried in "Ole Virginny *dirt*,"—rather a derogatory term to apply to the sacred soil that gave birth to the presidents—the soil of the Old Dominion.

Almost all of these letters told the same sad tale of destitution of food and clothing, even shoes of the roughest kind being either too expensive for the mass or unattainable by the expenditure of any sum, in many parts of the country. For the first two years of the war, privations were lightly dwelt upon and courageously borne, but when want and suffering pressed heavily as times grew more stringent, there was a natural longing for the stronger heart and frame to bear part of the burden. Desertion is a crime that meets generally with as much contempt as cowardice, and yet how hard for the husband or father to remain inactive in winter quarters, knowing that his wife and little ones were literally starving at home—not even *at home,* for few homes were left.

Our hospital had till now (the summer of 1863), been appropriated to the Gulf States, when an order was issued to transfer and make it entirely Virginian. The cause of this change was unknown, but highly agreeable, for the latter were the very best class of men in the field; intelligent, manly, and reasonable, with more civilized tastes and some desire to conform to rules that were conducive to their health. Besides this, they were a hardier race, and were more inclined to live than die,—a very important taste in a hospital,—so that when the summer campaigns were over, the wards would be comparatively empty.

The health of the army improved wonderfully after the first year's exposure had taught them to take proper precautions, and they had become accustomed to the roughnesses of field life. Time was given me, by this lightening of heretofore strenuous duties, to seek around and investigate the mysteries of the arrangements of other hospitals beside my own, and see how my neighbors managed their responsibilities. While on the search for material for improvement, I found a small body of Marylanders, who, having had no distinct refuge awarded them, were sent wherever circumstances made it convenient to lodge them.

There had been, from the breaking out of the war, much petty criticism, privately and publicly expressed, concerning the conduct and position of the Marylanders who had thrown their fortunes in the Confederate scale, and a great deal of ill-feeling engendered. Sister states have never been amicable, but it was not until my vocation drew my attention to the fact that I became aware of the antagonism existing. The Virginians complained that the Marylanders had come south to install themselves in the comfortable clerkships, and to take possession of the lazy places, while those filling them defended their position on the ground that efficient men were required in the departments, as well as the field, and that their superior capacity as clerks was recognized and rewarded without any desire, on their part, to shun field duty. They were unfortunate, as they labored under the disadvantage of harboring, as reputed fellow citizens, every gambler, speculator or vagabond, who, anxious to escape military duty, managed to procure, in some way, exemption papers proving him a native of their so-considered neutral state.

An adverse feeling towards them, report said, extended even to the hospitals through which they were scattered, and I endeavored long, but unsuccessfully, to induce Dr. Moore, the Confederate Surgeon-General, to inaugurate some building for their use. He was averse to any arrangement of this kind, not from prejudice, but a conviction of the expense and trouble of small establishments of this nature.

Not succeeding I made a personal application to the surgeon-in-chief of my own establishment, to allow me to appropriate a certain number of my own wards to them, and with the ready courtesy he always accorded me, he immediately gave consent.

In the decided objections of surgeons generally to taking charge of Marylanders there was an element more amusing than offensive, and the dismay of the head of our hospital when he heard of my arrangements was ludicrous in the extreme, and our opinions hardly reconcilable from our different standpoints. To a woman there was a touch of romance in the self-denial exercised, the bravery displayed and the hardships endured by a body of men, who were fighting for what was to them an abstract question, as far as they were concerned.

No one with any reasoning powers could suppose that Maryland in event of success could ever become a sister state of the Confederacy. Then the majority of them were very young men, who, well born, well nurtured and wealthy, accustomed too to all the luxuries of life, served then, and even to the end as privates, when less deserving men who had commenced their career in the ranks had made interest and risen, as much through political favor as personal bravery. Luxuries received from other states for their soldiers, which though trifling in themselves were so gratifying to their recipients could not come to them; the furlough, that El Dorado to the sick soldier, was the gold which could not be grasped, for there was no home that could be reached. Even letters, those electric conductors from heart to heart, came sparingly after long detention, often telling of the loss of the beloved at home, months after the grave had closed upon them.

In antagonism to these ideas were the strong objections of our head surgeon to this arrangement of mine, and they too were reasonable. The fact of there being an unusual amount of intelligence and independence among these men made them more difficult to manage, as they were less submissive to orders. They were aware of how much they were entitled to, in food, surgical and medical attendance and general comfort; and were not afraid to speak loudly and openly of neglect towards them or of incapacity in their rulers, so that whether ragged, helpless or sick they bore a striking resemblance to Hans Andersen's leather soldier. That historical personage, though lame in the leg, minus an arm and eye, with a mashed head, all the gilt rubbed off of his back and lying in a gutter, held his own opinion and gave it on all occasions.

The result of this was that there existed a pretty general objection to them as patients, as they were, to say the least, awkward customers. I might whisper an aside very low and confidential of sick men who should have followed the good old wholesome rule of "early to bed and early to rise" taking their physic obediently in the morning, but disappearing at night,—"dew in the morning and mist at night,"—and I might also tell of passes altered and furloughs lengthened when there was no fighting going on, all very wicked, but certainly nothing unmanly or dishonorable. They never lingered around when honor called, and their record needs no additional tribute from my humble pen. When sectional feelings shall have died away and a fair narration of the Confederate struggle be written, they will find their laurel leaves fresh and green.

But to return to domestic details. My new wards were prepared, freshly whitewashed, and adorned with cedar boughs for the reception of the old line Maryland cavalry, and during their sojourn I experienced to its fullest extent the pleasure of ministering to the wants of grateful and satisfied soldiers. They brightened a short interval of laborious and harassing labors that lasted over four years, and left a sunny spot for memory to dwell on. After their departure many more of their state came, generally infantry, and difficulties still continued. It was impossible to give them their due share of attention, so great was the feeling of jealousy existing. If an invalid required special attention, and he proved to be a Marylander, though perhaps ignorant myself of the fact, many eyes watched me, and complaints were made to the nurses, and from them to the surgeons, till a report of partiality to them on my part made to the surgeon-in-chief, called forth a remonstrance on his part, and a request that all patients should be treated alike. Then came an unpleasant season of bickering and dissatisfaction, so that fearing I might be to blame in part, I studiously at last avoided inquiring to what corps a man belonged.

A courier of General A. P. Hill's, very badly wounded, had been invalided for some time, and desirous of offering him some inducement to bear his fate more patiently, I had invited him to dine in my office, as soon as he could use his crutches. An invitation of this kind was often extended to men similarly situated; not that there were delicacies retained in my kitchen that did not reach the wards, but the request was a courtesy, and the food would be hot from the fire, and more comfortably served. Unfortunately he was a Marylander, and that some adverse report had been made was proved by an order attached to my window during the day, explaining that no patient would be permitted to enter the matron's department under any circumstances, on penalty of punishment. This was uncalled-far and galling, so I pulled it down first, and then carried my complaint to the surgeon-in-chief.

No one ever applied to him in vain for either justice or courtesy. He naturally was unwilling to countermand this order positively, but told me significantly that although the hospital was to a certain extent under the control of the surgeon in charge, and subject to his orders, the private rooms, as well as kitchen and laundry attached to the matron's department were under my management. As a woman will naturally sacrifice her comfort, convenience, pleasure, and privacy to have her own way, the result must be evident. My sleeping-room became a dining-room, and for the future I made what use of it I pleased, returning every night to my quarters at the Secretary's.

The next annoyance was the disappearance of all the Maryland patients; their wards being found empty one morning, and "no man living could tell where they had gone." However, when the flesh-pots of the forsaken land were steaming at dinner-time, a small group revealed themselves of the missing tribes, and clustered around my window with cup and plate. They belonged to the infantry, and seemed unable to bear their exile. This continued for a couple of days, the applicants increasing at each meal, till a second visit to Dr. McCaw with a representation of the impossibility of feeding men for whom no rations had been drawn brought about a rescinding of the order for their exile, and from that time they and all of their corps who came to me were unmolested.

CHAPTER 8

"A GROAN WAS SELDOM HEARD"

FEMININE sympathy being much more demonstrative than masculine, particularly when compared with a surgeon's unresponsiveness, who inured to the aspects of suffering, has more control over his professional feelings, the nurses often summoned me when only the surgeon was needed. One very cold night the same year, 1863, when sleeping at my hospital rooms, an answer was made to my demand as to who was knocking and what was wanted. The nurse from the nearest ward said, something was wrong with Fisher.

Instructing him to find the doctor immediately and hastily getting on some clothing I hurried to the scene, for Fisher was an especial favorite. He was quite a young man, of about twenty years of age, who had been wounded ten months previously very severely, high up on the leg near the hip, and who by dint of hard nursing, good food and plenty of stimulant had been given a fair chance for recovery. The bones of the broken leg had slipped together, then lapped, and nature anxious as she always is to help herself had thrown a ligature across, uniting the severed parts; but after some time the side curved out, and the wounded leg was many inches shorter than its fellow.

He had been the object of sedulous care on the part of all—surgeons, ward-master, nurse and matron, and the last effort made to assist him was by the construction of an open cylinder of pasteboard, made in my kitchen, of many sheets of coarse brown paper, cemented together with very stiff paste, and baked around the stove-pipe. This was to clasp by its own prepared curve the deformed hip, and be a support for it when he was able to use his crutches.

He had remained through all his trials, stout, fresh and hearty, interesting in appearance, and so gentle-mannered and uncomplaining that we all loved him. Supported on his crutches he had walked up and down his ward for the first time since he was wounded, and seemed almost restored. That same night he turned over and uttered an exclamation of pain.

Following the nurse to his bed, and turning down the covering, a small jet of blood spurted up. The sharp edge of the splintered bone must have severed an artery. I instantly put my finger on the little orifice and awaited the surgeon. He soon came—took a long look and shook his head. The explanation was easy; the artery was imbedded in the fleshy part of the thigh and could not be taken up. No earthly power could save him.

There was no object in detaining Dr. —. He required his time and his strength, and long I sat by the boy, unconscious himself that any serious trouble was apprehended. The hardest trial of my duty was laid upon me; the necessity of telling a man in the prime of life, and fullness of strength that there was no hope for him.

It was done at last, and the verdict received patiently and courageously, some directions given by which his mother would be informed of his death, and then he turned his questioning eyes upon my face.

"How long can I live?"

"Only as long as I keep my finger upon this artery." A pause ensued. God alone knew what thoughts hurried through that heart and brain, called so unexpectedly from all earthly hopes and ties. He broke the silence at last.

"You can let go—"

But I could not. Not if my own life had trembled in the balance. Hot tears rushed to my eyes, a surging sound to my ears, and a deathly coldness to my lips. The pang of obeying him was spared me, and for the first and last time during the trials that surrounded me for four years, I fainted away.

No words can do justice to the uncomplaining nature of the Southern soldier. Whether it arose from resignation or merely passive submission, yet when shown in the aggregate in a hospital, it was sublime. Day after day, whether lying wasted by disease or burning up with fever, torn with wounds or sinking from debility, a groan was seldom heard. The wounded wards would be noisily gay with singing, laughing, fighting battles o'er and o'er again, and playfully chaffing each other by decrying the troops from different states, each man applauding his own. When listening to them one would suppose that the whole Southern army with the exception of a few companies from the speaker's section of the country, were cowards.

The up-country soldiers, born in the same states as those they derided, went even further and decried "them fellows from the seaboard, who let us do all the fighting." The Georgians would romance of how the South Carolinians laid down at such a battle, refusing to charge, and how they had to "charge right over them." The Mississippians of the backwardness of the Tennessee troops, who "would never go into action unless led by their commanding general." The Virginians told bitter stories of the rowdy-

ism of the Maryland volunteers, who were "always spree-
ing it in the city, and dancing attendance on the women,"
and the North Carolinians caught it on all sides, though
their record is undoubtedly a most gallant one.

Taken in the mass, the last were certainly most forlorn
specimens, and their drawl was insufferable. Besides, they
never under any circumstances would give me the satisfaction of hearing that they relished or even ate any food
that was issued from my kitchen. "Say, can I have some
sweet soup?" whined a voice from one bed, and "Look
here, can I have some sour soup?" came from another.

The sweet soup upon explanation proved to be stirred
custard; the sour a mystery until the receipt was given.
"You jist put a crock of buttermilk on the fire, and let it
come to a bile; then mix up the yaller of an egg with
some corn flour to make a paste; then punch off pieces of
the dough, and bile them with the soup; with lots of
pepper and salt." The buttermilk when so tested by heat
resolved itself into a sea of whey with a hard ball of
curds in the center. I carried the saucepan to his bedside
to show the results of his culinary directions; but he merely
shook his head and remarked carelessly that "his mammy's
soup did not look like that."

Many would not eat unless furnished with food to
which they had been accustomed at home, and as unreas-
oning as brutes resisted nutriment and thus became weaker
day after day; and whatever was new to the eye or palate
was received suspiciously. Liquids in the form of soups,
tea or coffee they turned from with disgust, so that the
ordinary diet of invalids was inefficient in their case.
Buttermilk seemed especially created by nature for
wounded patients; they craved it with a drunkard's thirst,
and great, strong men have turned away from all else and
implored a drink of sweet milk.

We had a very short supply of this towards the end of the war, and I remember a stalwart Kentuckian, one of Morgan's men, insisting upon the rare luxury of one cupfull. He had been for many months on a raid far out of Confederate limits, and returning slightly wounded, had no idea of the scarcity of forage that made our cows so dry. His pleading became really affecting, till at last rallying, I told him: "Why man! the very babies of the Confederacy have given up drinking milk, and here are you, six feet two, crying for it."

Little poetical effusions were often thrust under my cabin door, and also notes of all kinds from my patients. Among them one day was a well-written and worded request from a young man who had been indisposed with that most hateful of all annoyances to soldiers—the itch; that shirt of Nessus, which when once attached to the person clings there pertinaciously. It begged me when at leisure to give him an interview, telling me his ward, name, and bed. He proved to be educated, and a gentleman from the upper part of Alabama, which had been colonized by the best class of South Carolinians; and he wished to enlist any influence I might possess in his favor, to endeavor to get him a furlough.

His story was interesting. Engaged to a young girl, the preparations made, the ring even bought (he wore it next his heart), and the marriage day fixed, they heard the first rumors of war, and patriotism urging him to enlist, the parents of his sweetheart naturally refused to allow him to consummate the engagement until peace was restored. The desire to see her again became almost unbearable, and feeling sincere sympathy with him, and the hardship of the case, I tried but in vain to have him furloughed. The campaign of 1864 had opened and every man was needed in the field.

The finale of my story is a sad one, as are almost all stories in time of war. He was killed while repelling with his brigade the attack on Petersburg, and the little history confided to me resolved itself into a romance one night, that found shape and form:

"ICH HABE GELEBT UND GELIEBT."

The bride's robe is ready, the bridesmaids are bid,
The groom clasps the circlet, so cautiously hid;
For a home is now waiting a mistress to claim
A lover, a wife, for his house, heart and name.
There is peace in the homestead and mirth in the hall—
The steed idly stands at his rack in the stall,
The whole land is teeming with prosperous life,
For lost are all memories of carnage and strife.
With rich golden harvest the ripe hills are blest,
And God's providence stands revealed and confessed.

  *   *   *   *   *   *   *   *

No priest blessed that union, no ring wed that hand;
With anger and discord soon rang the whole land;
Through all its wide domains the dread tidings rang
Of bloodshed. The lover was first in the van.
"My own one! I leave thee, those dear arms unfold.
Wouldst wed with the timid—the doubtful—the cold?
No union could bless till our country be free,
So onward for liberty, glory—and thee!"

  *   *   *   *   *   *   *   *

Right bravely fought he till sunlight lying low
Discovered a field that had left him no foe;
But when in the flush of a victory gained,
Deep in dreams of his love—his honor unstained,
He wended his way to the home of his heart
From her side ne'er to swerve, from her love ne'er to part,
Hast'ning on with his tidings he knew she would prize—
His heart on his lips and his soul in his eyes;
Laid low by a shot courage could not repel
At the feet of a mightier victor—he fell!
And the bride that he left? What needs it to say
Her doom was a woman's,—to watch, wait and pray.
The heat of the struggle nerves man for the strife,
But bitter at home is her battle of life,
When far from the conflict, unheeded, alone,
Her brain in a flame, but her heart like a stone,
She patiently waits to hear *one* life is won,
Or silently prays to say—*His* will be done!

CHAPTER 9

"THE WARS OF THE WHISKEY BARREL CONTINUED"

THE WHISKEY BARREL, as I have said before, and suppose I shall often say again, had been a bone of contention from the beginning, and as it afterward proved, continued so to the end. Liquor commanded an enormous price in Dixie, and often if its lovers had the means to procure it, the opportunity was wanting, as the hospital was some distance from Richmond. When first installed in my office, the desire to conciliate, and the belief that men generally had some conscience even on the whiskey question led me to yield to urgent solicitations for it from many quarters; but the demands increased fearfully upon any concession.

A reference to Dr. McCaw about this matter settled the heretofore open question. The doctor said the liquor was intended exclusively for the use of patients, and should only be used through a prescription accompanied by a written order. Also that I was personally responsible for the quantity confided to my care, and must each month produce the surgeon's receipts to balance with the number of gallons drawn from the medical purveyor.

There were at different times half a dozen surgeons and officials around, who absolutely made my life wretched by their importunities, and yet who could not be sent away except by preferring charges against them, and proving those charges; for my hospital was a military organization. I did not feel inclined to brave the publicity of preferred charges, for I seemed to have no recognized rank, and if even I could prove them, the complaints made would be ludicrously petty in detail, though distracting as mosquito bites in the aggregate.

The modes adopted to outflank me were named "legion." Some of them can be recalled. A quart bottle of whiskey would be ordered by the officer of the day for each ward, for night use, so that it would be ready at hand should any of the patients need this stimulant during the night. The next morning, on inquiry being made, there had been no case requiring its use, but the bottles would be empty, and expostulation on my part be met with explanations that the rats (who were a very plague), had knocked all the bottles over. On refusing to honor any more demands of the same kind, not believing in the rat story, the surgeon in charge would be appealed to, hear all sides, and favor none. This was just what I anticipated and wanted, for having, for the first few months of my occupation, lived in a state of active terror for fear of violating rules, however injurious the results of obeying, I recompensed myself from that time till the end of my sojourn by acting exactly as I thought right, braving the consequences and preferring to be attacked to attacking.

One mode of annoying me was particularly offensive— sending a negro boy with a cup and a simple request for whiskey, as if it was the most natural act in the world. At first a polite refusal would be written, but if this mode should have been persevered in, a private secretary would have been necessary; so in time it was replaced by a curt "No." A few minutes later the boy would again stand before me with the same message, and this would occur half a dozen times consecutively. I did not believe in vicarious punishment, so could not make the messenger responsible—he was compelled to obey; and sometimes, stung to irritation by this senseless pertinacity, I would write a note to the offending party, brief but sharp.

The reply would be the same silly question I so often had to meet: "Did Mrs. —— consider herself a lady when she wrote such notes?" "No," was always the indignant answer. "How could she be, when brought into contact with such elements?" It was strange, with so little outward self-assertion, always dressed in Georgia homespun, often the worse for wear, leather shoes, worsted gloves, and half the time with a skillet or coffee-pot in my hands, that all the common element around me should contest my right to a title to which I never aspired in words.

This fact, which must have been patent to them from the active persecution it entailed, seemed to be a crying grievance. My life at my hospital quarters when relieved from care for the patients was exclusive, from habit, inclination and prudence. Living a great part of my time away from all intercourse with my own sex, in a solitude that was unbroken after dark, it was better that no intimacies should be formed and no preferences shown; and in an exposed position where Argus eyes were always watching, a woman could not be too careful.

But still the wars of the whiskey barrel continued. One day the men of one of the distant wards sent for me in the absence of their wardmaster, and complained that the liquor issued for them never reached them. All concurred in this report, and said the champagne bottles in which it was kept were hid behind a certain vacant bed, from whence they would be abstracted that night. A search on my part brought them to light, still full, although the hour of administering had long past. The ward-master was summoned, the full bottles exhibited, and expressing my surprise at the inhumanity and dishonesty of one I had heretofore thought so honest, I warned him of the consequences that would result to him. His protestations were so earnest that he never tasted liquor, that I could not disbelieve him. What then had "become of the quantity issued, had he sold it?"

The charge was met by indignant surprise, and then the truth began to dawn upon me. That he had been false to his charge and his patients was true, if even he had not been guilty of taking it, and I warned him that on my representing the matter to the proper authorities he would be sent to the field. An hour after this conversation the surgeon of his ward entered my office with belligerent aspect.

"Did you assert, Madam, that you intended sending my ward-master to the field?"

"I said I intended laying the facts concerning the disappearance of the liquor before the proper authorities."

"I consider myself responsible, Madam, for the liquor used in my wards."

"If you do, you fail to be sure that it reaches its destination, so I intend in future to see that it does."

"If you mean that my ward-master drinks it, you are mistaken; he does not take any stimulant."

"I know he does not," I answered quietly, "and I also know who does."

He changed color, and passing him I walked into my little sanctum adjoining the office. To my astonishment he kicked back the door and also entered.

"Doctor, this is my private room," I said, "to which no one is admitted. Be kind enough to leave."

"Not until you explain," he answered, throwing himself at full length upon the couch.

This was just far enough for him to venture. I threw back my window, and called to the sentry to order up a sergeant and file of the guard. In a few minutes the ring of their muskets outside sounded, and taking out my watch, I placed it on the table by him.

"I will give you five minutes," I said, "to leave my room. If you are not gone by that time, commissioned officer as you are, and gentleman as you ought to be, I will have you taken to the guard-house, and then explain this matter to the surgeon-general."

He waited a minute or two, soliloquizing audibly that I must fancy myself the Secretary of War, and he would make me know my position, but soon made up his mind that discretion was the better part of valor, and left. Proper measures were no doubt taken to punish such conduct, for though I made no complaint, there were no secrets in a hospital, and after a few weeks he disappeared, sent no doubt to that Botany Bay—"the front." He took a gallant leave of his associates, hinting that his talents demanded a wider field of action than a hospital.

But the tables were about to be turned. Not forever would I be allowed to carry war into the enemy's country, or be the sole defender of that friend by whom I had stood so gallantly. The whiskey barrel was destined after all to be turned into a weapon of offense.

The bold man who thus declared hostilities and by a *coup-de-guerre* changed the whole nature of the war from offensive to defensive tactics, had been bar-keeper in a Georgia tavern, afterwards a clerk in a Macon dispensary, in order to escape field duty. Coming to Richmond he passed the board of surgeons by a process known only to themselves, which often rejected good practitioners, and gave appointments to apothecary boys.

Fate sent him to our hospital, where the brilliant idea struck him to check thefts of whiskey in the feminine department. He inaugurated his plans by ordering a pint of it for a single patient.

The etiquette of a hospital enjoins that no one but the chief surgeon shall dispute an inferior surgeon's prescription, so I carried this generous order to the chief, received his instructions not to exceed the usual "from two to four ounces" without being served with a formal requisition signed by the surgeon in charge, and so I wrote this gentleman (a contract surgeon) a few lines, courteously explanatory of my reasons for so cutting him down. This matter being arranged, I forgot all about it, but the next day the blow was struck; the following note being handed to me:

"HOSPITAL, Richmond, April 3, 1864.

"The Chief Matron:—Is respectfully asked to state the amount of water used as compared with amount of whiskey in making toddy. Also if strength of toddy has been uniform since January 1st, 1863. Also if any change has taken place in diluting within the same period. She will also state what the change has been; also when made, and by whose authority.   Respectfully,

"................................ ....,

"Assistant Surgeon in charge."

These questions, if even he had any right to ask them (which he had not), were simply absurd. With hundreds of men requiring different drinks many times each day, ordered by numerous surgeons, prepared to suit different stages of disease and palate, no hour bringing the same orders, how could any kind of a correct statement be made, even if I was willing to make it? But there was a great deal of amusement in the idea of letting him suppose he had alarmed me. Perhaps, as the day was very wet, and the wards rather empty, we might enact a small comedy; so I sat down and answered in full, respectfully, feeling very charitably that he was welcome to all the information he could extract from the five closely-written sheets of foolscap I despatched him.

In this document, polite, officially formal and as officially obscure, I thought I had succeeded in showing my correspondent that his questions could not be answered satisfactorily, but that I was much alarmed at his asking them. That I did not succeed in regard to his first inquiry was proved by the following, which came after an hour's delay.

"HOSPITAL, April 3rd, 1864.

"Chief Matron:—Is respectfully called upon to state what amount of whiskey has been given to each patient when amount has not been stated or expressed by surgeon, or assistant surgeon, upon the rolls, but instead 'whiskey three times a day,' and shown upon the rolls which *I* send *you*.

"Respectfully,

"...................... ....,

"Assistant Surgeon in charge."

No solemn pages greeted him in answer this time. My rejoinder was concise and to the point.

"HOSPITAL, April 3rd, 1864.

"The Chief Matron regrets that she is too busily engaged to give any more voluminous explanations, being at this moment up to her elbows in gingerbread."

Then the sleeping lion was roused, for almost instantly the reply was brought me, and an alarming finale it was.

"Hospital, April 3rd, 1864.

"Chief Matron: Is hereby informed that if she willfully and contumaciously refuses to give me such information as I demand, and she is possessed of, thereby obstructing the duty I feel myself called upon to perform, she must be prepared to *meet* the responsibility upon *your own shoulders.*

"Respectfully,

" ....,

"Assistant Surgeon in charge."

A serious but sharp rejoinder sent to this gentleman, trying to show him that he had no authority to propound these questions, closed this paper war; and I had forgotten all about the matter, when the correspondence was forwarded me, folded in official style, and indorsed at the surgeon-general's office on the back "Referred respectfully to the surgeon-in-chief—Hospital," through whose hands alone official etiquette required all reports should pass to heads of departments. He had courteously sent it to me, and I as courteously sent it to the forwarder.

Seeing that he had failed to interest the surgeon-general in the case, he drew up a statement of the affair, accusing me of disrespect (based upon the gingerbread letter particularly) to my *superior officer,* sending it accompanied by all the obnoxious notes to the office of the military governor of the department of Henrico, who I heard read it all with some amazement—if not interest.

Back, however, it came shortly again without response, and by this time some of the waggish surgeons having been made confidants in the matter, persuaded my dis-

appointed friend to try the Secretary of War; and at one
of the charming breakfasts which his wife was in the habit
of giving, I saw him with a smile draw from his pocket
a package I knew well by that time, and made my escape
just in time to avoid hearing it all over again. As I
mounted the ambulance in waiting to take me to my hospital, I heard the peals of laughter that greeted the reading of those unlucky documents.

My acquaintance with my correspondent was never
renewed. He kept out of my way. The only time I ever
saw him again was the day he left and I viewed his pan-
taloons of Georgia clay embrowning the landscape adown
the hill.

A better educated class of surgeons was sent to fill
fortunate vacancies, and this change made my duties more
agreeable. There would have been nothing disagreeable
in the occupation I had assumed if a proper discretion had
been exercised, or proper rules enforced, so that no
demands should have been made upon the matron for
that which she had no right to give. These demands were
the beginning and end of my troubles; for in all else
except complying with them I tried hard not to exceed
the duties of my position, and succeeded so well that no
temptation could induce me to interfere in any way with
medical treatment, not even to offering the slightest
alleviation to suffering men.

During my early initiation, when quite a novice, yield-
ing to a poor fellow's prayer for something to wash a
mouth frightfully excoriated by calomel I gave him a few
drops of myrrh in water, and suffered the annoyance of
seeing it contemptuously tossed out of the window by the
assistant surgeon. From that day I made up my mind to
resist all such impulses and persevered in the same line
of conduct to the end.

But antagonism was not always the rule. There were many sensible, kind-hearted efficient men among the surgeons who gave their time and talents generously to further the comfort and well-being of their patients,—men who would let me work hand in hand with them, the nurse with the doctor, and listen kindly and respectfully to my suggestions, if they were not calculated to benefit science.

As I have said, the chief surgeon was an unfailing refuge in times of distress, and whenever broken down by fatigue and small miseries I sought his advice and assistance, the first was not only the very best that could be secured, but unlike most of its kind, palatable; and the last entirely efficient.

The surgeon, too, of my hospital [division], though eccentric and wanting in decision of character, sustained my authority during sore trials as ably as he could; for the power delegated to him was not great, and his dread of responsibility a disease. He never intended to be unjust or unkind, but self-examination and investigation of characters around him was not his forte. He certainly withstood a vast amount of complaint directed against his chief matron; and while we had our pleasant little difficulties occasionally, that we still preserved amicable relations was due more to his amiable temper than my proper submission. I *think* he had many faults, but I am sure I had more, and if the popular remark which has since become a maxim, that a man must be very clever to "keep a hotel" be true, it certainly ought to apply to one who can govern a hospital.

CHAPTER 10

INTENSIFICATION OF SUFFERING
AND HATRED

Now during the summer of 1864 began what is really meant by "war," for privations had to be endured which tried body and soul, and which temper and patience had to meet unflinchingly day and night. A growing want of confidence was forced upon the mind; and with doubts which though unexpressed were felt as to the ultimate success of our cause, there came into play the antagonistic qualities of human nature.

The money worthless, and a weak Congress and weaker financier failing to make it much more valuable than the paper it was printed on; the former refusing to the last to raise the hospital fund to meet the depreciation. Everything furnished through government contracts of the very poorest description, perhaps necessarily so from the difficulty of finding any supply.

The railroads were cut so constantly that what had been carefully collected in the country in the form of poultry and vegetables by hospital agents would be rendered unfit for use by the time the connection would be restored. The inducements for theft were great in this season of scarcity of food and clothing. The pathetic appeals made for the coarsest meal by starving men, all wore upon the health and strength of those exposed to the strain, and made life weary and hopeless.

The rations became so small about this time that every ounce of flour was valuable, and there were days when it was necessary to refuse with aching heart and brimming eyes the request of decent, manly-looking fellows for a piece of dry corn-bread. If given it would have robbed the rightful owner of part of his scanty rations. After the flour or meal had been made into bread, it was almost ludicrous to see with what painful solicitude Miss G. and myself would count the rolls, or hold a council over the pans of corn-bread, measuring with a string how large we could afford to cut the squares, to be apportioned to a certain number.

Sometimes when from the causes above stated, the supplies were not issued as usual, invention had to be taxed to an extreme, and every available article in our pantry brought into requisition. We had constantly to fall back upon dried apples and rice for convalescing appetites, and herb-tea and arrowroot for the very ill. There was only one way of making the last at all palatable, and that was by drenching it with whiskey.

Long abstinence in the field from everything that could be considered, even then, a delicacy, had exaggerated the fancy of sick men for any particular article of food they wanted into a passion; and they begged for such peculiar dishes that surgeons and nurses might well be puzzled. The greatest difficulty in granting these desires was that tastes became contagious, and whatever one patient asked for, his neighbor and the one next to him, and so on throughout the wards, craved also, and it was impossible to decide upon whom to draw a check.

No one unacquainted with our domestic relations can appreciate the difficulties under which we labored. Stoves in any degree of newness or usefulness we did not have; they were rare and expensive luxuries. As may be supposed, they were not the most convenient articles in the world to pack away in blockade-running vessels; and the trouble and expense of land transportation also seriously affected the quality of the wood for fuel, furnished us. Timber which had been condemned heretofore as unfit for use, light, soggy and decayed, became the only quality available. The bacon, too, cured the first two years of the war, when salt commanded an enormous price, in most cases was spoilt, from the economy used in preparing that article; and bacon was one of the sinews of war.

We kept up brave hearts, and said we could eat the simplest fare, and wear the coarsest clothing, but there was absolutely nothing to be bought that did not rank as a luxury. It was wasting time and brain to attempt to economize, so we bent to the full force of that wise precept, "Sufficient for the day is the evil thereof."

There really was a great deal of heroism displayed when looking back, at the calm courage with which I learned to count the number of mouths to be fed daily, and then contemplating the food, calculate not how much but how little each man could be satisfied with. War may be glorious in all its panoply and pride, when in the field opposing armies meet and strive for victory; but battles fought by starving the sick and wounded—by crushing in by main force day by day all the necessities of human nature, make victories hardly worth the name.

Another of my local troubles were the rats, who felt the times, and waxed strong and cunning, defying all attempts to entrap them, and skillfully levying blackmail upon us day by day, and night after night. Hunger had educated their minds and sharpened their reasoning faculties. Other vermin, the change of seasons would rid us of, but the coldest day in winter, and the hottest in summer, made no apparent difference in their vivacious strategy.

They examined traps with the air of connoisseurs, sometimes springing them from a safe position, and kicked over the bread spread with butter and strychnine to show their contempt for such underhand warfare. The men related wonderful rat-stories not well enough authenticated to put on record, but their gourmands ate all the poultices applied during the night to the sick, and dragged away the pads stuffed with bran from under the arms and legs of the wounded.

They even performed a surgical operation which would have entitled any of them to pass the board. A Virginian had been wounded in the very center of the instep of his left foot. The hole made was large, and the wound sloughed fearfully around a great lump of proud flesh which had formed in the center like an island. The surgeons feared to remove this mass, as it might be connected with the nerves of the foot, and lock-jaw might ensue. Poor Patterson would sit on his bed all day gazing at his lame foot and bathing it with a rueful face, which had brightened amazingly one morning when I paid him a visit. He exhibited it with great glee, the little island gone, and a deep hollow left, but the wound washed clean and looking healthy.

Some skillful rat surgeon had done him this good service while in the search for luxuries, and he only knew that on awaking in the morning he had found the operation performed. I never had but one personal interview with any of them. An ancient gray gentleman, who looked a hundred years old, both in years and depravity, would eat nothing but butter, when that article was twenty dollars a pound; so finding all means of getting rid of him fail through his superior intelligence, I caught him with a fish-hook, well baited with a lump of his favorite butter, dropped into his domicile under the kitchen floor.

Epicures sometimes managed to entrap them and secure a nice broil for supper, declaring that their flesh was superior to squirrel meat; but never having tasted it, I cannot add my testimony to its merits. They staid with us to the last, nor did I ever observe any signs of a desire to change their politics.

Perhaps some curious *gourmet* may wish a recipe for the best mode of cooking them. The rat must be skinned, cleaned, his head cut off and his body laid open upon a square board, the legs stretched to their full extent and secured upon it with small tacks, then baste with bacon fat and roast before a good fire quickly like canvas-back ducks.

One of the remarkable features of the war was the perfect good nature with which the rebels discussed their foes. In no instance up to a certain period did I hear of any remark that savored of personal hatred. They fought for a cause and against a power, and would speak in depreciation of a corps or brigade; but "they fit us, and we fit them," was the whole story generally, and till the blowing up of the mine at Petersburg there was a gay, insouciant style in their descriptions of the war scenes passing under their observation.

But after that time the sentiment changed from an innate feeling the Southern soldiers had that mining was "a mean trick," as they expressed it. They were not sufficiently versed in military tactics to recognize that strategem is fair in war, and what added to their indignation was the pouring in of *negro* soldiers when the breach was effected. Incensed at the surprise, they craved foes worthier of their steel, not caring to rust it in the black cloud that issued from the crater. The men had heretofore been calm and restrained, particularly before a woman, never using oaths or improper language, but the wounded that were brought in from that fight emulated the talents of Uncle Toby's army in Flanders, and eyes gleamed, and teeth clenched as they showed me the locks of their muskets to which the blood and hair still clung, when after firing, without waiting to re-load, they had clenched the barrels and fought hand to hand. If their accounts could be relied upon, it was a gallant strife and a desperate one, and ghastly wounds bore testimony of the truth of many a tale then told.

Once again the bitter blood showed itself, when, after a skirmish, the foe cut the rail track, so that the wounded could not be brought to the city. Of all the monstrous crimes that war sanctions, this is surely the most sinful. Wounded soldiers without the shelter of a roof, or the comfort of a bed of straw, left exposed to sun, dew, and rain, with hardly the prospect of a warm drink or decent food for days, knowing that comfortable quarters awaited them, all ready prepared, but rendered useless by what seems an unnecessarily cruel act. Was it any wonder that their habitual indifference to suffering gave way, and the soldier cursed loud and deep at a causeless inhumanity, which, if practiced habitually, is worse than savage! When the sufferers at last reached the hospital, their wounds had not been attended to for three days, and the sight of them was shocking.

Busy in my kitchen, seeing that the supply of necessary food was in preparation, I was spared the sight of much of the suffering, but on passing among the ambulances going in and out of the wards I descried seated up in one of them a dilapidated figure, both hands holding his head which was tied up with rags of all descriptions. He appeared to be incapable of talking, but nodded and winked and made motions with head and feet. In the general confusion he had been forgotten, so I took him under my especial charge. He was taken into a ward, seated on a bed, while I stood on a bench to be able to unwind rag after rag from around his head. There was no sensitiveness on his part, for his eye was merry and bright, but when the last came off, what a sight!

Two balls had passed through his cheek and jaw within half an inch of each other, knocking out the teeth on both sides and cutting the tongue in half. The inflammation caused the swelling to be immense, and the absence of all previous attendance, in consequence of the detention of the wounded until the road could be mended, had aggravated the symptoms. There was nothing fatal to be apprehended, but fatal wounds are not always the most trying.

The sight of this was the most sickening my long experience had ever seen. The swollen lips turned out, and the mouth filled with blood, matter, fragments of teeth from amidst all of which the maggots in countless numbers swarmed and writhed, while the smell generated by this putridity was unbearable. Castile soap and soft sponges soon cleansed the offensive cavity, and he was able in an hour to swallow some nourishment he drew through a quill.

The following morning I found him reading the newspaper, and entertaining every one about him by his abortive attempts to make himself understood, and in a week he actually succeeded in doing so. The first request distinctly enunciated was that he wanted a looking-glass to see if his sweetheart would be willing to kiss him when she saw him. We all assured him that she would not be worthy of the name if she would not be delighted to do so.

An order came about this time to clear out the lower wards for the reception of improperly-vaccinated patients, who soon after arrived in great numbers. They were dreadfully afflicted objects, many of them with sores so deep and thick upon arms and legs that amputation had to be resorted to, to preserve life. As fast as the eruption would be healed in one spot, it would break out in another, for the blood seemed entirely poisoned. The unfortunate victims bore the infliction as they had borne everything else painful—with calm patience and indifference to suffering. Sometimes a favorable comparison would be made between this and the greater loss of limbs.

No one who was a daily witness to their agonies from this cause, can help feeling indignant at charges made of inhumanity to Federal prisoners of war, who were vaccinated with the same virus; and while on this subject, though it may be outside of the recollections of hospital life, I cannot help stating that on no occasion was the question of rations and medicines to be issued for Federal prisoners discussed in my presence; and circumstances placed me where I had the best opportunity of hearing the truth (living with the wife of a cabinet officer); that good evidence was not given, that the Confederate commissary-general, by order of the government issued to them the same rations it gave its soldiers in the field, and only when reductions of food had to be made in our army, were they also made in the prisons. The question of supplies for them was an open and a vexed one among the people generally, and angry and cruel things were *said;* but every one cognizant of facts in Richmond *knows* that even when General Lee's army lived on corn-meal at times that the prisoners still received their usual rations.

At a cabinet meeting when the Commissary-General Northrop advocated putting the prisoners on the half rations which our soldiers had been obliged to content themselves with for some time, General Lee opposed him on the ground that men animated by companionship and active service could be satisfied with less than prisoners with no hope and leading an inactive life. Mr. Davis sided with him, and the question was settled that night, although in his anger Mr. Northrop accused General Lee of showing this consideration because his son was a prisoner in the enemy's lines.

CHAPTER 11

VISITORS STAY AND STAY—AND MULTIPLY

MY HOSPITAL was now entirely composed of Virginians and Marylanders, and the nearness to the homes of the former entailed upon me an increase of care in the shape of wives, sisters, cousins, aunts, and whole families including the historic baby at the breast. They came in troops, and hard as it was to know how to dispose of them, it was harder to send them away. Sometimes they brought their provisions with them, but not often, and even when they did there was no place for them to cook their food. It must be remembered that everything was reduced to the lowest minimum, even fuel. They could not remain all day in the wards with men around them, and if even they were so willing, the restraint on wounded, restless patients who wanted to throw their limbs about with freedom during hot summer days, was unbearable.

Generally their only idea of kindness was giving sick men what food they would take in any quantity and of every quality, and in the furtherance of their views they were pugnacious in the extreme. Whenever rules circumscribed their plans they abused the government, then the hospital and then myself.

Many ludicrous incidents happened daily, and I have often laughed heartily at seeing the harassed ward-master heading away a pertinacious female who failing to get

past him at one door would try the three others persever-
ingly. They seemed to think it a pious and patriotic duty
not to be afraid or ashamed under *any* circumstances. One
sultry day I found a whole family accompanied by two
young lady friends seated around a wounded man's bed;
as I passed through six hours later, they held the same
position.

"Had not you all better go home?" I said good-
naturedly.

"We came to see my cousin," answered one very
crossly. "He is wounded."

"But you have been with him all morning, and that is
a restraint upon the other men. Come again tomorrow."

A consultation was held, but when it ceased no movement was made, the older ones only lighting their pipes
and smoking in silence.

"Will you come back tomorrow, and go now?"

"No! You come into the wards when you please, and
so will we!"

"But it is my duty to do so. Besides, I always ask permission to enter, and never stay longer than fifteen
minutes at a time."

Another unbroken silence, which was a trial to any
patience left, and finding no movement made, I handed
some clothing to a patient near.

"Here is a clean shirt and drawers for you, Mr. Wilson;
put them on as soon as I get out of the ward."

I had hardly reached my kitchen, when the whole procession, pipes and all, passed me solemnly and angrily;
but for many days, and even weeks, there was no ridding
the place of this large family connection. Their sins were
manifold. They overfed their relative who was recovering
from an attack of typhoid fever, and even defiantly seized

the food for the purpose from under my very nose. They marched on me *en masse* at ten o'clock at night, with a requisition from the boldest for sleeping quarters. The steward was summoned, and said "he didn't keep a hotel," so in a weak moment of pity for their desolate state, I imprudently housed them in my laundry. They entrenched themselves there for six days, making predatory incursions into my kitchen during my temporary absences, ignoring Miss G. completely.

The object of their solicitude recovered and was sent to the field, and finding my writs of ejectment were treated with contemptuous silence, I sought an explanation. The same spokeswoman alluded to above, met me half-way. She said a battle was imminent she had heard, and she had determined to remain, as her husband might be wounded. In the ensuing press of business she was forgotten, and strangely enough, her husband was brought in with a bullet in his neck the following week.

The back is surely fitted to the burden, so I contented myself with retaking my laundry, and letting her shift for herself, while a whole month slipped away. One morning my arrival was greeted with a general burst of merriment from everybody I met, white and black. Experience had made me sage, and my first question was a true shot, right in the center.

"Where is Mrs. Daniells?" (she who had always been spokeswoman).

"In ward G. She has sent for you two or three times."

"What is the matter now?"

"You must go and see."

There was something going on, either amusing or amiss. I entered ward G, and walked up to Daniells' bed. One might have heard a pin drop.

I had supposed, up to this time, that I had been called upon to bear and suffer every annoyance that humanity and the state of the country could inflict; but here was something most unexpected in addition; for lying composedly on her husband's cot (he had relinquished it for the occasion) lay Mrs. Daniells, and her baby, just two hours old.

The conversation that ensued is not worth repeating, being more of the nature of soliloquy. The poor little wretch had ventured into a bleak and comfortless portion of the world, and its inhuman mother had not provided a rag to cover it. No one could scold her at such a time, however ardently they might desire to do so. But what was to be done? I went in search of my chief surgeon, and our conversation although didactic was hardly satisfactory on the subject.

"Doctor, Mrs. Daniells has a baby. She is in ward G. What shall I do with her?"

"A baby! Bless me! Ah indeed! You must get it some clothes."

"What must I do with *her?*"

"Move her to an empty ward and give her some tea and toast."

This was offered, but Mrs. D. said she would wait until dinner-time and have some bacon and greens.

The baby was a sore annoyance. The ladies of Richmond made up a wardrobe, each contributing some article, and at the end of the month, Mrs. D., the child, and a basket of clothing and provisions were sent to the cars with a return ticket to her home in western Virginia. My feelings of relief can be imagined. But the end had not come. An hour after the ambulance had started with them, it stopped at my kitchen door apparently empty, and the black driver with a grin half of delighted mischief and half of fear silently lifted a bundle out and deposited it carefully upon my kitchen dresser. Mrs. Daniells' baby!

The unnatural woman had deserted it, leaving it in the railroad depot, but the father fortunately was still with us and to him I appealed. A short furlough was obtained for him, and he was despatched home with his embarrassing charge and a quart of milk. He was a wretched picture of helplessness, but had I sent again for the mother I should never have got rid of her. It may be remarked *en passant* that she was not wholly ungrateful, for the baby was named after me.

There were no means of keeping the relations of patients from coming to them. There had been rules made to meet their invasion, but it was impossible to carry them out, as in the instance of a wife wanting to remain with her husband; and besides even the better class of people looked upon the comfort and care of a hospital as a farce. They resented the detention there of men who in many instances could lie in bed and point to their homes within sight, and argued that they would have better attention and food if allowed to go to their families.

That *maladie du pays* called commonly nostalgia, the home-sickness which wrings the heart and impoverishes the blood, killed many a brave soldier; and the matron who day by day had to stand helpless and powerless by the bed of the sufferer, knowing that a week's furlough would make his heart sing for joy, and save his wife from widowhood, learned the most bitter lesson of endurance that could be taught.

This home-sickness recognized no palliation. However carefully the appetite might be pampered, or stimulants prepared and given, the food never nourished, the drink never strengthened; the decay would be gradual, but death was inevitable. Perhaps when recovery seemed hopeless, a statement of the case might procure a furlough from the examining board of surgeons, but the patient would then be too weak and low to profit by the concession. It was wonderful to see how long the poor broken machine would hold out in some cases. For months I have watched a victim, helpless, hopeless and motionless, simply receive into his mouth daily a few spoonfuls of nourishment, making no other movement, the skin barely covering the bones, and the skeleton of the face as sharply defined as it might have been days after dissolution. The answer to cheering words seldom exceeding a slight movement of the eyelids.

Towards the end of the war, this detention of men who could have been furloughed at first, and some other abuses were reformed by allowing a board to be convened of three of the oldest surgeons attached to the hospital, who had authority to dispose of such cases without deferring to higher powers. There had been so much imposition practiced by men desirous of getting furloughs, and so many abuses had crept in despite the stringency of rules, that severity seemed necessary.

CHAPTER 12

RICHMOND IMPERILLED

THE SPRING CAMPAIGN of 1864 again opened with the usual "On to Richmond." Day after day and night after night would the sudden explosion of cannon boom upon the air. The enemy were always coming, and curiosity seemed to have usurped the place of fear among the women. In the silence of night the alarm bells would suddenly peal out, till the order to ring them at any sign of danger was modified to a command to sound them only in case of positive attack. The people became so accustomed to the report of firearms, that they scarcely interrupted their conversation at corners of the streets to ask in what direction the foe was advancing, or if there was any foe at all.

There was such entire reliance upon the military vigilance that guarded the city, and former attacks had been so promptly repelled, that whatever was ultimately to be the result of the war, no one trembled then for Richmond. So the summer of 1864 passed, and early in September our hearts were gladdened by the tidings that the exchange of prisoners was to be renewed. The sick and wounded of our hospital (but few in number just then) were transferred to other quarters, and the wards put in order to receive our men from Northern prisons.

Can any pen or pencil do justice to those squalid pictures of famine and desolation? Those gaunt, lank skeletons with the dried yellow flesh clinging to bones enlarged by dampness and exposure? Those pale, bluish lips and feverish eyes, glittering and weird when contrasted with the famine-stricken faces,—that flitting, piteous, scared smile which greeted their fellow creatures, all will live forever before the mental vision that then witnessed it.

Living and dead were taken from the flag-of-truce boat, not distinguishable save from the difference of care exercised in moving them. The Federal prisoners we had released were in many instances in a like state, but our ports had been blockaded, our harvests burned, our cattle stolen, our country wasted. Even had we felt the desire to succor, where could the wherewithal have been found? But the foe,—the ports of the world were open to him. He could have fed his prisoners upon milk and honey, and not have missed either. When we review the past, it would seem that Christianity was but a name—that the Atonement had failed, and Christ had lived and died in vain.

But it was no time then for vague reflections. With beating heart, throbbing head and icy hands I went among this army of martyrs and spectres whom it was almost impossible to recognize as human beings; powerless to speak to them, choking with unavailing pity, but still striving to aid and comfort. There was but little variety of appearance. From bed to bed the same picture met the eye. Hardly a vestige of human appearance left.

The passion of sympathy could only impede my efforts if yielded to, for my hand shook too tremulously even to allow me to put the small morsels of bread soaked in wine into their mouths. It was all we dared to give at first. Some lay as if dead with limbs extended, but the greater part had drawn up their knees to an acute angle, a position they never changed until they died. Their more fortunate comrades said that the attitude was generally assumed, as it reduced the pangs of hunger and relieved the craving that gnawed them by day and by night. The Federal prisoners may have been starved at the South, we cannot deny the truth of the charge, in many instances; but we starved with them; we had only a little to share with any—but the subject had better be left to die in silence.

One among them lingered in patience the usual three days that appeared to be their allotted space of life on their return. He was a Marylander, Richard Hammond Key, grandson of Francis Barton Key, author of "Star Spangled Banner," and hence heir to a name renowned in the history of his country. Though reared in affluence, he presented the same bluish, bloodless appearance common to all the returned prisoners. Hoping that there would be some chance of his rallying, I gave him judicious nursing and good brandy. Every precaution was taken, but the third day fever supervened and the little life left waned rapidly. He gave me the trinkets cut from gutta percha buttons that he had beguiled his captivity in making at Point Lookout, to send to his family, handing me one of them for a souvenir; begged that he might be buried apart from the crowd in some spot where those who knew and cared for him might find him some day, and quietly slept himself to death that night.

The next morning was the memorable 29th September, 1864, when the enemy made a desperate and successful attack, taking Fort Harrison, holding it and placing Richmond in jeopardy for four hours. The alarm bells summoned the citizens together, and the shops being closed to allow those who kept them to join the city guards, there were no means of buying a coffin, or getting a hearse. It was against the rules to keep a body beyond a certain time on the hospital grounds, so little time was to be lost if I intended keeping my promise to the dead.

I summoned a convalescent carpenter from one of the wards, made him knock together a rough coffin from some loose boards, and taking the seats out of my ambulance had it, with the body enclosed, put in. My driver was at his post with the guards, so taking the reins and kneeling in the little space at the side of the coffin I started for Hollywood cemetery, a distance of five miles.

The enemy were then in sight, and from every elevated point the masses of manœuvering soldiers and flash of the enemy's cannon could be distinguished. Only stopping as I passed through the city to buy a piece of ground from the old cemetery agent, I reached Hollywood by twelve o'clock. Near the burying ground I met the Reverend J. D. McCabe, requested his presence and assistance, and we stood side by side while the sexton dug his grave. The rain was pouring in torrents, while the clergyman repeated the Episcopal burial service from memory. Besides ourselves there were but two poor women, of the humblest class of life—Catholics, who passing casually, dropped upon their knees, undeterred by the rain, and paid their humble tribute of respect to the dead.

He had all the honors of a soldier's burial paid to him unconsciously, for the cannon roared and the musketry rattled, mingling with the thunder and lightning of Heaven's artillery. The sexton held his hat over the small piece of paper on which I inscribed his name and birthplace (to be put on his headboard) to protect it from the rain, and with a saddened heart for the solitary grave we left behind I drove back to the city. The reverend gentleman was left at his home, and, perhaps, to this day does not know who his companion was during that strange hour.

I found the city in the same state of excitement, for no authentic news was to be heard, or received, except perhaps at official quarters; and it was well known that we had no troops nearer than Petersburg, save the citizens who had enrolled themselves for defense; therefore, too anxious to return directly to the hospital, I drove to the residence of one of the cabinet ministers, where I was engaged to attend a dinner, and found the mistress of the establishment, surrounded by her servants and trunks preparing for a hasty retreat when necessary. Some persuasion induced her to desist, and the situation of the house commanding an extensive view of the surrounding country, we watched the advance of the enemy from the extreme northeast, for with the aid of opera-glasses we could even distinguish the colors of their uniforms. Slowly onward moved the bodies of dark blue, emerging from and disappearing into the woods, seeming to be skirting around them, but not to be diminishing the distance between, although each moment becoming more distinct, which proved their advance, while not one single Confederate jacket could be observed over the whole sweep of ground.

Half an anxious hour passed, and then, far away against the distant horizon, one single mounted horseman emerged from a thick wood, looked cautiously around, passed across the road and disappeared. He was in gray, and followed by another and another, winding around and cutting off the foe. Then a startling peal at the bell, and a courier brought the news that Wade Hampton and his cavalry were close upon the rear of the enemy. There

was no occasion for fear after this, for General Hampton
was the Montrose of the Southern army, he who could
make any cause famous with his pen and glorious with
his sword. The dinner continued in course of preparation,
and was seasoned, when served, by spirits brightened by
the strong reaction.

CHAPTER 13

INCIDENTS OF HOSPITAL LIFE IN 1864

THE HORRORS that attended, in past times, the bombardment of a city, were experienced in a great degree in Richmond during the fighting around us. The close proximity to the scenes of strife, the din of battle, the bursting of shells, the fresh wounds of the men hourly brought in were daily occurrences. Walking through the streets during this time, after the duties of the hospital were over, when night had well advanced, the pavement around the railroad depot would be crowded with wounded men just brought in, and laid there waiting for conveyance to the receiving hospitals. Some on stretchers, others on the bare bricks, or laid on a thin blanket, suffering from wounds hastily wrapped around with strips of coarse, unbleached, galling bandages of homespun cotton, on which the blood had congealed and stiffened until every crease cut like a knife.

Women passing accidentally, like myself, would put down their basket or bundle, and ringing at the bell of neighboring houses, ask for basin and soap, warm water, and a few soft rags, and going from sufferer to sufferer, try to alleviate with what skill they possessed, the pain of fresh wounds, change the uneasy posture, and allay the thirst. Others would pause and look on, till the labor appearing to require no particular talent, they too would

103

follow the example set them, and occasionally asking a word of advice, do their duty carefully and willingly.

Idle boys would get a pine knot or tallow-dip, and stand quietly and curiously as torch-bearers, till the scene, with its gathering accessories formed a strange picture, not easily forgotten. Persons driving in different vehicles would alight sometimes in evening dress, and choosing the wounded most in need of surgical aid, put them in their places, and send them to their destination, continuing their way on foot. There was little conversation carried on, no necessity for introductions, and no names ever asked or given. This indifference to personality was a peculiarity strongly exhibited in hospitals, for after nursing a sick or wounded patient for months, he has often left without any curiosity exhibited as regarded my name, my whereabouts, or indeed any thing connected with me.

A case in point was related by a friend. When the daughter of our general had devoted much time and care to a sick man in one of the hospitals, he seemed to feel so little gratitude for the attention paid, that her companion to rouse him told him that Miss Lee was his nurse. "Lee, Lee?" he said. "There are some Lees down in Mississippi who keep a tavern there. Is she one of them Lees?"

Almost of the same style, although a little worse was the remark of one of my sick, a poor fellow who had been wounded in the head and who, though sensible enough ordinarily, would feel the effect of the sun on his brain when exposed to its influence. After advising him to wear a wet paper doubled into the crown of his hat more from a desire to show some interest in him than from any belief in its efficacy, I paused at the door long enough to hear him ask the ward-master "who that was?" "Why, that is the matron of the hospital; she gives you all the food you eat, and attends to things." "Well!" said he, "I always did think this government was a confounded sell and now I am sure of it, when they put such a little fool to manage such a big hospital as this."

The ingenuity of the men was wonderful in making toys and trifles, and a great deal of mechanical talent was developed by the enforced inaction of hospital life. Every ward had its draught-board and draughtsmen cut out of hard wood and stained with vegetable dies, and sometimes chessmen would be cut out with a common knife, in such ornamentation that they would not have disgraced a drawing-room. One man carved pipes from ivy root, with exquisitely-cut shields on the bowls, bearing the arms of the different states and their mottoes. He would charge and easily get a hundred and fifty dollars for a pipe (Confederate paper was then sixty cents for the dollar), and he only used his well-worn pocket-knife.

Playing cards—the greatest comfort to alleviate the tedium of their sick life—were difficult to get a substitute for, so that the original packs had a hard time. They became, as may be supposed from the hands which used them, very dirty in a short time, and the corners in a particularly disreputable condition, but after the diffusion of the Oxford editions of the different books of the Bible sent from England as a donation, the soldiers took a lesson, and rounded the corners in imitation. A pack of cards after four years' use in a Southern hospital was beyond criticism.

The men had their fashions, too, sometimes insisting upon having light blue pants drawn for them, and at other seasons preferring gray; but while the mania for either color raged, they would be dissatisfied with the other. When the quartermaster-general issued canvas shoes, there was a loud dissatisfaction expressed in constant grumbling, till some original genius dyed the whitish tops by the liberal application of poke-berries. He was the Brummel of the day, and for many months crimson shoes were the rage, and long rows of unshod men would sit under the eaves of the wards, all diligently employed in the same labor and up to their elbows in red juice.

This fashion died out, and gave place to a button mania. Men who had never had a dream or a hope beyond a horn convenience to keep their clothing together, saved up their scanty means to replace them with gilt, and made neat little wooden shelves with a slit through the middle into which the buttons slid, so that they could be cleaned and brightened without taking them off, or soiling the jacket. With the glitter of buttons came the corresponding taste for gilt bands and tinsel around the battered hat, so that while our future was lowering darker and darker, our soldiers were amusing themselves like children who had no interest in the coming results.

The duty which of all others pressed most heavily upon me and which I never did perform voluntarily was that of telling a man he could not live, when he was perhaps unconscious that there was any danger apprehended from his wound. The idea of death so seldom occurs when disease and suffering have not wasted the frame and destroyed the vital energies, that there is but little opening or encouragement to commence such a subject unless the patient suspects the result ever so slightly. In many cases, too, the yearning for life was so strong that to destroy the hope was beyond human power. Life was for him a furlough, family and friends once more around him; a future was all he wanted, and considered it cheaply purchased if only for a month by the endurance of any wound, however painful or wearisome.

There were long discussions among those responsible during the war, as to the advisability of the frequent amputations on the field, and often when a hearty, fine-looking man in the prime of life would be brought in minus an arm or leg, I would feel as if it might have been saved, but experience taught me the wisdom of prompt measures. Poor food and great exposure had thinned the blood and broken down the system so entirely that secondary amputations performed in the hospital almost invariably resulted in death, after the second year of the war. The blood lost on the battlefield when the wound was first received would enfeeble the already impaired system and render it incapable of further endurance.

Once we received a strong, stalwart soldier from Alabama, and after five days' nursing, finding the inflammation from the wound in his arm too great to save the limb, the attending surgeon requested me to feed him on the best I could command; by that means to try and give him strength to undergo amputation.

Irritability of stomach as well as indifference to food always accompanying gun-shot wounds, it was necessary, while the fever continued, to give him as much nourishment in as small a compass as possible, as well as easily digestible food, that would assimilate with his enfeebled condition. Beef tea he (in common with all soldiers and I believe men) would not, or could not take, or anything I suggested as an equivalent, so getting his consent to drink some "chemical mixture," I prepared the infusion.

Chipping up a pound of beef and pouring upon it a half pint of water, the mixture was stirred until all the blood was extracted, and only a teaspoonful of white fibre remained; a little salt was added, and favored by the darkness of the corner of the ward in which he lay, I induced him to swallow it. He drank without suspicion, and fortunately liked it, only complaining of its being too sweet; and by the end of ten days his pulse was fairly good, and there had been no accession of fever. Every precaution was taken, both for his sake and the benefit of the experiment, and the arm taken off by the most skillful surgeon we had.

After the amputation, which he bore bravely, he looked as bright and well as before, and so on for five days— then the usual results followed. The system proved not strong enough to throw out the "pus" or inflammation; and this, mingling with the blood, produced that most fatal of all diseases, pyæmia, from which no one ever recovers.

He was only one of numerous cases, so that my heart beat twice as rapidly as ordinarily whenever there were any arrangements progressing for amputation, after any length of time had elapsed since the wound, or any effort made to save the limb. The only cases under my observation that survived were two Irishmen, and it was really so difficult to kill an Irishman that there was little cause for boasting on the part of the officiating surgeons. One of them had his leg cut off in pieces, amputation having been performed three times, and the last heard from him was that he had married a young wife and settled on a profitable farm she owned in Macon, Georgia.

He had touched the boundary lines of the "unknown land," had been given up by the surgeons, who left me with orders to stimulate him if possible. The priest (for he was a Catholic) was naturally averse to my disturbing what he considered the last moments of a dying man who had made his confession and taken his farewell of this world, and which ought to have been devoted to less worldly temptations than mint juleps; and a rather brisk encounter was the result of a difference of opinion on the subject; for if he was responsible for the soul, so was I for the body, and I held my ground firmly.

It was hard for an Irishman and a good Catholic to have to choose at this supreme moment between religion and whiskey; but though his head was turned respectfully towards good Father T—— his eyes rested too lovingly on the goblet offered to his lips to allow me to make any mistake as to the results of his ultimate intentions. The interpretation put by me on that look was that Callahan thought that as long as first proof brandy and mint lasted in the Confederacy this world was good enough for him, and the result proved that I was not mistaken. He always gave me the credit I have awarded to the juleps, and until the evacuation of Richmond kept me informed of his domestic happiness.

CHAPTER 14

A TRAIN TRIP TO GEORGIA,
OCTOBER, 1864

T HOUGH my health up to this time had withstood the bad effects of exposure and exertion, the strain had become too great, and the constantly recurring agitation which had been excited each day on receiving the returned prisoners, had broken me down completely. A visit to the surgeon-general with a request for a month's leave of absence, met with a ready acquiescence. The old gentleman was very urbane, even making one or two grim jokes, and handed me not only permission to leave, but the necessary transportation. Very necessary in this case, as traveling expenses were enormously high, and the government had seized for the whole month of October the railroads for military use, putting a complete stop to private travel.

It had been like tearing body and soul apart, when necessity compelled me to leave my hospital, from which I had never been separated but one day in nearly four years; and when all arrangements for departure had been completed, Miss G. urged, entreated and commanded to keep a sharp look-out upon the whiskey, and be alike impenetrable to feints, strategems and entreaties, my heart began to sink.

A visit to the wards did not tend to strengthen my wavering resolves. The first invalid to whom I communicated the news of my intended departure burst into a passion of tears, and improved my frame of mind by requesting me to kill him at once, for he would certainly die if left. Standing by his bedside, unsettled and irresolute, all the details of my daily life rose before me. The early and comforting visit to the sick after their feverish, restless night; when even if there were no good to be effected, they would feel the kindness, and every man's head would be thrust out of the bed-clothes as by one impulse, and jealousy evinced when a longer pause by one bedside than another would arouse the feeling. Often has the ward-master recalled me when at the distance of a quarter of a mile from his ward, at the request of a patient, and when going back to find out what was wanted, a hearty convalescent would explain that I had passed through and omitted to speak to him.

Farewells were exchanged at last, and the 6th October, 1864, found me at the Fredericksburg station, *en route* for Georgia. A search at the last moment before stepping into the cars, discovered that my keys, together with my watch, had been left at the hospital, while, as an equivalent, there remained at the bottom of my basket half a salt mackerel (a rare luxury in the Confederacy), begged for a sick man who fancied it, a day before, and forgotten in the hurry of packing. I was compelled to defer my start until the 7th.

There are some schoolday recollections hanging around the softening by Hannibal of a rugged journey by the plentiful application of vinegar; but what acid could soften the rigors of that trip to Georgia? They can hardly be recounted in any degree of limited space. With the aid of two gentlemen, and indeed every disengaged man on the road, a safe termination was effected after many days, and a delicious holiday passed in idleness and

Confederate luxury, free from the wear and tear of constantly excited feelings.

Then came the stern reflection that I had no right to exceed the furlough of thirty days accorded by Dr. Moore. A search was immediately made for an escort, which having failed, general advice was unanimously given to "go alone," on the grounds that women had become entirely independent at this time, and "no man knowing the object of your journey could fail to give you all the assistance you would need."

Fired with this Quixotic sentiment, an early start was made. Finding almost immediately that I had not received checks for my trunks, I ventured, while the afflatus lasted, to touch a man who sat in front of me on the arm, and request him to call the conductor. "I am sorry to say that I am not acquainted with him," was the answer; and down I went to zero, never rising again till my journey was accomplished.

Perhaps the details of my trials may give my readers some idea of the state of the country at that time. At West Point, which took an hour and a half's travel to reach from LaGrange we had to sleep all night, there being no connection for twelve hours. There were no bedrooms, and no candles to be had, and the female travelers sat in the little bar of the tavern (the leading hotel being closed) brightened by a pine knot, with their feet on the sanded floor, and ate what they had provided themselves with from their baskets.

Another two hours' travel on to Opelika the next day, and another detention for half-a-dozen hours. At Columbus, a rumor that the cars had been seized for government transportation made me anxious concerning the nature of my ticket, which I found to my dismay was not suited to meet the emergency through some inadvertence; so long before starting-time I was waiting at the depot seated on my trunk, half amused and half mortified at the resemblance thus offered to an emigrant Irish servant woman.

The place was crowded with invalided soldiers, for the government was moving the hospitals to the lower part of the state, and idle spectators seeing my evident alarm offered all kinds of irrational advice. A suggestion was sensibly made by some one that by seeking one of the most helpless of the wounded and requesting him to allow me to pass as his nurse my object might be effected; but every man to whom I opened my proposals seemed alarmed at and opposed to this idea. Towards the last the confusion became distracting—everybody calling for the conductor, who possessing no power, the cars being under military control, first denied his identity and then hid himself.

Help came at the last moment in the form of a red-faced, half-tipsy Irish porter who had been cheering me on with winks of encouragement at my frantic efforts for some time. "Lit me put yer trunks on," he said, and "thin go to Colonel Frankland at the rare of the cars—sure he's the man to help the faymales."

My forlorn hope, Colonel Frankland, was standing on the platform at the extreme rear of the cars, surrounded by a semi-circle below, about twenty-five feet deep, all pressing on to get to seats already too full. He was gesticulating and shouting like a madman. The lame, the halt, and the blind stood around. Crutches, splints, and huge sticks represented a small wood. Green blinds over eyes, raw faces peeled from erysipelas, and still showing variegated hues of iodine, gave picturesqueness to the scene. Had he borne Cæsar and his fortunes he could not have been more interested. For two hours he had been stemming this living tide.

I had met and fraternized with a lady and gentleman, old acquaintances, encountered at the depot, who appeared as anxious to get Northward as myself; so telling her not to move until I had either achieved my object or failed, and if I made her a sign to join me, I took my position at the fag end of the crowd below the colonel, and undeterred by distance and uproar I essayed a faint call for notice. The sound died away in my throat, but my Irish friend (I am sure he took me for one of his cousins from the "ould counthrie") was by my side in an instant and repeated the call. A hundred voices took up the refrain, "A lady wants to speak to the colonel," and universal curiosity regarding the *private* nature of my business being exhibited by a profound silence I raised my voice as Mause Headrigg said, "like a pelican in the wilderness:"

"Colonel Frankland, I must get forward on this train tonight. Government business requires me to be in Richmond by the 1st November."

"Can't do it, Madam. Would like to oblige you, but can't go against my orders. The cars are for the use of sick and wounded soldiers alone."

"But Colonel Frankland, hundreds of invalids are waiting for their breakfast, dinner and supper in Richmond. I am the matron of —— hospital."

"Can't help it, Madam! If you men there don't keep away from this platform and leave a passage way, I'll put the front rank under arrest!"

"Oh! Colonel Frankland, cannot I stand on the platform, if I am not allowed to use the cars?"

"No, Madam, it would be dangerous. Sorry to refuse."

"Let me go in the freight train."

"There is no freight train."

"Well, the box cars? I take very little room."

"They are crowded, Madam, crowded. Keep off, men, keep off there!"

The steam blew and whistled fearfully and the bell clanged an uproar of sound. A passing car came rushing by and my courage was oozing fast. "Try him agin!" said my Irish friend, who unable to get near me, shouted his secret.

"Oh! Colonel Frankland, excuse my pertinacity, but what *can* I do? Let me go on in the mail car! I will not even open my eyes to look at the outside of the letters."

"Against the law. Cannot be done. How can I infringe upon my orders? Will no one keep those confounded men off?"

"*I will,* Colonel Frankland, if you will let me get up by your side. I will keep every single man away. Now men, keep off, I beg of you, for I must get to Richmond, and moreover, I wear very long hair-pins."

"Thank you, Madam, thank you. Now men, you hear what this lady says, and I know she will be as good as her word." A hundred hands helped me up. I looked for my friend, the red-nosed Irishman, but he was gone. Another moment and my friend stood by my side, assisted by the Irishman, who tipped me a comprehensive wink which set my mind at rest as regarded the safety of my trunk.

"This is not fair," said the Colonel. "You promised that no one should get on."

"Oh, no, I promised that not a *single man* should do so. This is a woman. Will you let her husband join her? He is not a *single* man, for he has a wife and nine children!"

The result may be imagined. Our party, very much relieved, were soon inside, where we found four comfortable seats reserved for General Beauregard and staff, which were unoccupied from these gentlemen being detained at Macon.

At that city, where we were compelled to pass the night, the same state of things existed, and with depressed spirits I drove to the cars to see if any arrangement could be effected by which I could pursue my journey. The road would not be opened to the traveling public for a month, so an effort had to be made. An appeal to the authorities resulted as I expected, in defeat, so I again tried my manœuver of trying to interest subordinates.

Failing, however, and baffled at every turn, while sitting again upon my trunk, the mail agent, standing in the doorway of his car, caught my eye. Improving the opportunity, I commenced a conversation, ending in an insinuating appeal to be taken into the mail box. Success and installation in his little square domicile followed, and my friend, passing out without any explanation, locked the door on the outside. There were no windows and no light whatever; the hour six in the evening. Seated in loneliness and darkness till the town clock struck eight, every fear that could arise in the brain of a silly woman assailed me. Did the train I was in go to Augusta, and if not, would I be left where I was all night? Was the man who locked me up the mail agent? If he came back and robbed and murdered me, would any one ever miss me? Having had nothing to eat but a couple of biscuits in twenty-four hours, and my brain being, in consequence, proportionately light, imagination seized the reins from common sense, which fled in the presence of utter darkness and loneliness.

At last the key turned in the lock, and the light of a lantern dispelled some of my terrors. The cars started and the agent commenced sorting his letters, first bolting us in securely. A couple of hours passed and my mind was gradually losing its tone of unpleasant doubt as to the wisdom of my proceedings, when my busy companion knocked off work and essayed to play the agreeable. He was communicative in the extreme, giving me his biography, which proved him to be a Connecticut man, and very much dissatisfied with the Confederacy, particularly with the state of the money market. So long as he kept to his personal recollections all was right, but he soon claimed a return of confidence, and grew hourly more patronizing and conversational.

His tone and manner, the loneliness of the position, and the impossibility of any fortunate interruption occurring becoming unbearable at last, there is no knowing what I might have ventured to do, in the way of breaking out, if the cars had not fortunately run off the track. On we bumped, happily on level ground, for two minutes or more; the engineer entirely unconscious of the fact and no way of communicating with him, as the soldiers were lying over the rope on the top of the cars, so that pulling was in vain. At last a pause, and then a crowd, and then a familiar name was called, most welcome to my ears. I repeated it aloud until the owner was by my side, and the rest of the night was spent in asking questions and receiving information. At daylight he left me to rejoin his command, while we continued on to Augusta.

As usual, when we arrived there no vehicle of any kind met us at the depot. Since I was the only woman in the cars, the mail driver offered me a seat upon the mail-bags, and as it was raining I accepted, and in this august style reached the hotel by breakfast time. All military suspension ceased here, but there was detention for two hours, and this was enlivened by an amusing episode at the depot.

Directly in front of me sat an old Georgia up-country woman, placidly regarding the box cars full of men on the parallel rails, waiting like ourselves to start. She knitted and gazed, and at last inquired "who was them ar soldiers, and whar was they a-going to?" The information that they were Yankee prisoners startled her considerably. The knitting ceased abruptly (all the old women in the Southern states knitted socks for the soldiers while traveling), and the Cracker bonnet of dark brown homespun was thrown back violently, for her whole nervous system seemed to have received a galvanic shock. Then she caught her breath with a long gasp, lifted on high her thin, trembling hand, accompanied by the trembling voice, and made them a speech:

"Ain't you ashamed of you-uns," she piped, "a-coming down here a-spiling our country, and a-robbing our hen-roosts? What did we ever do to you-uns that you should come a-killing our brothers and sons? Ain't you ashamed of you-uns? What for do you want us to live with you-uns, you poor white trash? I ain't got a single nigger that would be so mean as to force himself where he warn't wanted, and what do we-uns want with you? Ain't you ———" but here came a roar of laughter from both cars, and shaking with excitement the old lady pulled down her spectacles, which in the excitement she had pushed up on her forehead, and tried in vain to resume her labors with uncertain fingers.

From here to Richmond there occurred the usual detentions and trials of railroad travel under the existing circumstances. The windows of the cars were broken out in many places. Sometimes no fire for want of stoves, and the nights damp and chilly. All in utter darkness, for the lamps were gone, and could they have been replaced, there would have been no oil.

We crawled along, stopping every hour almost, to tin-
ker up some part of the car or the road, getting out at
times when the conductor announced that the travelers
must walk "a spell or two," meaning from one to five
miles. Crowds of women were getting in and out all the
way, the male passengers grumbling aloud that "women
had better stay at home, they had no business to be
running around in such times."

This was said so often that it became very unpleasant,
till the tables were turned early one morning at Gains-
borough, when a large-sized female made her way along
the center of the car, looking from right to left in the
vain search for a seat. None being vacant, she stopped
short, and addressed the astonished male passengers with
more vigor than elegance: "What for pity sake do you
men mean by running all around the country for, instead
of staying in the field, as you ought to do? You keep filling up the cars so that a woman can't attend to her business. Your place should be opposite the enemy." This
diversion on our behalf was received silently, but many
seats were soon vacated by their occupants on the plea of
"taking a little smoke."

At last, the 1st of November found me weary, hungry,
cold and exhausted by travel at the Richmond depot, four
hours after schedule time; with that most terrible scourge,
a bad, nervous headache racking me all over. The crowd
around was immense, so that by the time it opened and
dispersed sufficiently to let me make my way through,
every vehicle had left, if there had ever been any there
before. As usual, my telegram had not been received, so
there was no one to meet me, and pain rendering me
indifferent to appearances I quietly spread my shawl upon
a bench and myself upon it.

For how long I cannot say, but I was roused by a voice asking what I wanted, and what was the matter? "Any kind of a vehicle to take me home," was the answer. After a few moments' delay my new friend returned with the information that there was only a market cart, which if I was willing to ride in, was for hire. If it had been a hearse it would have been hailed with welcome. My two trunks were put on, and I was deposited on them. The hour, eleven at night.

I looked first at the horse. He had a shadowy gray skin stretched over his prominent bones, and in the dim, misty light, seemed a mere phantom. The driver next came under observation. A little dried-up, gray black, old darkey, with a brown rag tied around his head, but like all his species he was kindly disposed and respectful. Directions were given him to drive to a friend's house. He said that his horse was too tired, but if I were willing, he had another "at his place," where he would drive me and change.

Quite willing, or rather too weary to assert any authority, so on we rumbled and rattled almost twice the distance I was first bound, changed one skeleton for another, and started again for my friend's house. At last the blessed haven was reached, but the sight of a new face to my summons at the door made my heart sink. She had "moved yesterday."

"Drive to Miss G.'s house," was my next direction, intending to throw myself upon her hospitality and charity for the night, for we were out of the way of all hotels.

The same result on application. Had all Richmond moved? The fresh air, and the necessity for exertion in this novel position had routed my headache, and now gave me courage to make a proposition I hadn't dared to make before.

"Could not you drive me to the hospital on the hill?" was my demand made in most ingratiating tones.

The old man untied the rag from off his head, and smoothed it on his knee by way of ironing out the creases and assisting reflection; replaced it, taking up the reins again before he answered, for we were now at a stand-still at the Broad Street hill.

"Missis," said he solemnly, "de way it is long, and de bridges dey is rotten; but ef you is not afeared to dribe ober dem by you-self, and let me git out, and pay me ten dollars, de ole hoss might be consarned to go up dis yere hill."

The bargain was struck, and the hospital reached after midnight. The key of my apartments sent for, when the duplicate hair that at last broke the camel's back was laid upon mine.

"Miss G. had taken it with her."

"Bring a carpenter," I cried desperately; "and tell him to get a sledge-hammer and knock down, or in, anything that will let me get into the place. I *must* have rest."

The door was broken open; a fire was kindled; a delicious piece of cold hard cornbread found and devoured, and when the warm covering of the first bed I had slept in for ten days was drawn around me, all the troubles of a hard world melted away, and the only real happiness on earth, entire exemption from mental and bodily pain, took possession of me.

CHAPTER 15

A TIPSY SURGEON SETS THE WRONG LEG

I NOTICED on my return a great difference in the means of living between Virginia and the Gulf States. Even in the most wealthy and luxurious houses in Richmond, former everyday comforts had about this time become luxuries, and had been dispensed with earlier in the war.

Farther south, they still received from Nassau what they needed, always running the risks of losing the cargoes of the blockade-runners, therefore duplicating orders. Tea and coffee were first given up at the capital, then many used corn flour,—wheat was so high. Gradually butter disappeared from the breakfast table, and brown sugar when it reached twenty dollars a pound shared the same fate. But no such economy appeared necessary where I had been. The air of the people in the cars and around the railroad stations was hopeful in the extreme. There was no doubt expressed even at this late day, the November of 1864, as to the ultimate success of the Southern cause.

Their hospitals though did not compare with those I had left in Virginia, either in arrangement, cleanliness or attendance. Even as early as 1862 the matrons' places there had been filled by ladies of education and refinement; but this with a few exceptions had been the rule in Virginia only, and such supervision made a marked difference, as may be supposed.

During my absence, the greater portion of the patients I had left a month previously had either recovered and left, or died, so that it was awkward to resume my duties among strangers. A few days' visiting rectified this however. The happiest welcome I got was from Miss G., who resigned the key of the liquor closet with a sigh which spoke volumes. From what could be gathered, she had been equal to the occasion, and knowing the hardship of her dragonship I did not press her strenuously upon points connected with it.

The health of the army was now so good, that except when the wounded were sent in, we were comparatively idle. That terrible scourge, pneumonia, so prevalent early in the war, and so fatal in its typhoid form, had almost disappeared. The men had become accustomed and inured to exposure. Christmas passed pleasantly. The hospital fund (from the great depreciation of the money) being too small to allow us to make much festive preparation, the ladies of the city drove out in carriages and ambulances laden with good things. The previous years we had been enabled to give out of the expenditure of our own funds a bowl of eggnogg and a slice of cake, for lunch, to every man in the hospital, as well as his portion of turkey and oysters for dinner; but times were more stringent now.

Soon after New Year, 1865, some members of the committee on hospital affairs called to see me, desirous of getting some information regarding the use or abuse of liquor, before the bill for the appropriations for the coming year would be introduced. There were doubts afloat as to whether the benefit conferred upon the patients by the use of stimulants counterbalanced the evil effects they

produced on the surgeons, who were in the habit of
making use of them when they could get them.

The problem was difficult to solve. A case in point had
lately come under my observation. A man had been
brought into our hospital with a crushed ankle, the cars
having run over it. He had been attended to, and the leg
put in splints before we had received him, so as he was
still heavy and drowsy, possibly from some anodyne
administered, the surgeon in attendance ordered him to
be left undisturbed. The nurse in a few hours came to me
to say that the man was suffering intensely. He had a
burning fever, and complained of the fellow leg instead
of the injured one.

The natural idea of sympathy occurred, and a sedative
given which failed in producing any effect. I determined
to look at it in spite of orders, his sufferings appearing so
great, and finding the foot and leg above and below the
splint perfectly well, the thought of examining the fellow
leg suggested itself. It was a most shocking sight—
swollen, inflamed and purple—the drunken surgeon had
set the wrong leg!

The pain induced low fever, which eventually assumed
a typhoid form, and the man died. With this instance
fresh in my memory I hesitated to give any opinion in
favor, and yet felt we could not manage without the
liquor. However, the appropriation was made.

This poor fellow was the most dependent patient I
ever had, and though entirely uneducated, won his way
to my sympathies by his entire helplessness and belief in
the efficacy of my care and advice. No surgeon in the hospital could persuade him to swallow anything in the shape
of food unless I sanctioned the order, and a few kindly
words, or an encouraging nod would satisfy and please
him.

His ideas of luxuries were curious, and his answer to my daily inquiries of what he could fancy for food, was invariably the same—he would like some "scribbled eggs and flitters." This order was complied with three times daily, until the doctor prescribed stronger food and though many dainties were substituted, he still called them by the same name, leading me to suppose that "scribbled eggs and flitters" was his generic term for food. I made him some jelly, Confederate jelly—with the substitution of whiskey for Madeira wine, and citric acid for lemons, but he said "he did not like it, there was no chewing on it," and "it all went, he did not know where!" so I gave up trying to tempt his palate.

When whole wards would be emptied of their occupants, in compliance with changes made to suit certain views of the surgical department, and strangers put in, I would always feel a great repugnance to visiting them. But when the change became gradual, by the convalescents, in twos or threes or half-dozens, being exchanged for invalids, there would always be enough men left to whom I was known, to make me feel at home, and to inform the newcomers why I came among them, and what my duties were.

I now found my hospital filled with strangers. They were not so considerate as my old friends had been, and looked rather with suspicion upon my daily visits. One man amused me particularly by keeping a portion of his food every day for my special and agreeable inspection, as he thought, and my particular annoyance, as I felt. A specimen of everything he thought unpalatable was deposited under his pillow, to await my arrival, and the greeting invariably given me was:

"Do you call that good bread?"

"Well no, not very good; but the flour is very dark and musty."

Another day he would draw out a handful of dry rice.

"Do you call *that* properly boiled?"

"That is the way we boil rice in Carolina. Each grain must be separated."

"Well! I won't eat mine boiled that way."

And so on through all the details of his food. Somebody he felt was responsible, and unfortunately he determined that I should be the scapegoat. His companion who lay by his side was even more disagreeable than he was. Being a terrible pickle consumer, he indulged in such extreme dissipation in that luxury that a check had to be put upon his appetite. He attacked me upon this grievance the first chance he found, and listened scornfully to my remarks that pickles were luxuries to be eaten sparingly and used carefully. "Perhaps," he said at last, "we would have more pickles if you had fewer new dresses." There was no doubt that I wore a new homespun dress, but what connection it had with the pickles was rather mysterious. However, that afternoon came a formal apology, written in quite an elegant style, and signed by every man in the ward, except the pickle man, in which the fault of this cruel speech was laid upon the bad whiskey.

CHAPTER 16

COLLAPSE OF THE CONFEDERACY

ALL THIS WINTER of '64, the city had been unusually gay. Besides parties, private theatricals and tableaux were constantly exhibited. Wise and thoughtful men disapproved openly of this mad gayety. There was certainly a painful discrepancy between the excitement of dancing and the rumble of ambulances that could be heard in the momentary lull of the music, carrying the wounded to the different hospitals. Young men advocated this state of affairs, arguing that after the fatigues and dangers of a campaign in the field, some relaxation was necessary on their visits to the capital.

To thinking people this recklessness was ominous; and by the end of February, 1865, it began to be felt by them that all was not as safe as it was supposed to be. The incessant moving of troops through the city from one point to another proved weakness, and the scarcity of rations issued told a painful tale. People rated the inefficiency of the commissary department, and predicted that a change in its administration would make all right. Soon afterwards the truth was told me in confidence and under promise of strict secrecy. Richmond would be evacuated in a month or six weeks. The time might be lengthened or shortened, but the fact was established.

Then came the packing up, quietly but surely, of the different departments. Requisitions on the medical pur-

127

veyor were returned unfilled, and an order from the
surgeon-general required that herbs instead of licensed
medicines should be used in the hospitals. There was a
great deal of merriment elicited from the "yarb teas,"
drawn during this time by the surgeons; few knowing the
sad cause of their substitution.

My mind had been very unsettled as to my course of
action in view of the impending crash, but my duty
prompted me to remain with my sick, on the ground that
no general ever deserts his troops. But to be left by all
my friends to meet the dangers and privations of an
invested city, among antagonistic influences, with the
prospect of being turned out of my office the next day
after the surrender, was not a cheering one. Even my
home would no longer be open to me; for staying with
a cabinet minister, he would leave with the government.
I was spared the necessity of decision by the sudden attack
of General Grant, and the breaking of the Confederate
lines, and before there was time to think at all, the government and all its train had vanished.

On the 2nd of April, 1865, while the congregation of
Dr. Charles Minnegerode's church in Richmond were
listening to his Sunday sermon, a messenger entered and
handed a telegram to Mr. Davis, President of the Confederate States, who rose immediately, and without any
visible signs of agitation or surprise, left the church. No
alarm was exhibited by the congregation, though several
members of the president's staff followed him, till Dr.
Minnegerode brought the service to an abrupt close, and
informed his startled flock that the city would be evacuated
shortly, and they would only exercise a proper degree of
prudence by going home immediately, and preparing for
the event.

This announcement, although coming from such a reliable source, hardly availed to convince the Virginians that their beloved capital, assailed so often, defended so bravely, surrounded by fortifications on which the engineering talents of their best officers had been expended, was to be capitulated. Some months before, a small number admitted behind the veil of the temple had been apprised that the sacrifice was to be accomplished; that General Lee had again and again urged Mr. Davis to yield this Mecca of his heart to the interests of the Confederacy, and resign a city which required an army to hold it, and pickets to be posted from thirty to forty miles around it, weakening his depleted army; and again and again had the iron will triumphed, and the foe, beaten and discomfited, retired for fresh combinations and fresh troops

But the hour had come, and the evacuation was only a question of time. Day and night had the whistle of cars proved to the anxious people that brigades were being moved to strengthen this point or defend that; and no one was able to say exactly where any portion of the army of Virginia was stationed. That Grant would make an effort to strike the Southside railroad—the main artery for the conveyance of food to the city—every one *knew;* and that General Lee would be able to meet the effort and check it, everybody *hoped,* and while this hope lasted there was no panic.

The telegram which reached Mr. Davis that Sunday morning, was to the effect that the enemy *had* struck, and on the weakest point of the Confederate lines. It told him to be prepared in event of the repulse failing. Two hours after came the fatal news that Grant had forced his way through, and that the city must instantly be evacuated. What is meant by that simple sentence "evacuation of the city" but few can imagine who have not experienced it.

The officials of the various departments hurried to their offices, speedily packing up everything connected with the government. The quartermaster's and commissary's stores were thrown open and thousands of the half-starved and half-clad people of Richmond rushed to the scene.

Delicate women tottered under the weight of hams, bags of coffee, flour and sugar. Invalided officers carried away articles of unaccustomed luxury for sick wives and children at home. Every vehicle was in requisition, commanding fabulous remuneration, and gold or silver the only currency accepted. The immense concourse of government employes, speculators, gamblers, strangers, pleasure and profit lovers of all kinds that had been attached to that great center, the Capital, were "packing," while those who had determined to stay and await the chances of war, tried to look calmly on, and draw courage from their faith in the justness of their cause.

The wives and families of Mr. Davis and his cabinet had been sent away some weeks previously, so that no provision had been made for the transportation of any particular class of people. All the cars that could be collected were at the Fredericksburg depot, and by 3 o'clock P.M. the trains commenced to move.

The scene at the station was of indescribable confusion. No one could afford to abandon any article of wear or household use, when going where they knew that nothing could be replaced. Baggage was as valuable as life, and life was represented there by wounded and sick officers and men, helpless women and children, for all who could be with the army were at their post.

Hour after hour fled and still the work went on. The streets were strewn with torn papers, records and documents too burdensome to carry away, too important to be left for inspection, and people still thronged the thoroughfares, loaded with stores until then hoarded by the government and sutler shops.

The scream and rumble of the cars never ceased all that weary night, and was perhaps the most painful sound to those left behind, for all the rest of the city seemed flying; but while the center of Richmond was in the wildest confusion, so sudden had been the shock that the suburbs were quiet and even ignorant of the scenes enacting in the heart of the city. Events crowded so rapidly upon each other that no one had time to spread reports.

There was no change in the appearance of the surroundings till near midnight, when the school-ship, the *Patrick Henry,* formerly the old United States ship *Yorktown,* was fired at the wharf at Rocketts, the extreme eastern end of the city. The blowing up of her magazine seemed the signal for the work of destruction to commence. Explosions followed from all points. The warehouses and tobacco manufactories were fired, communicating the flames to the adjacent houses and shops, and soon Main Street was in a blaze. The armory, not intended to be burnt, either caught accidentally or was fired by mistake; the shells exploding and filling the air with hissing sounds of horror, menacing the people in every direction. Colonel Josiah Gorgas had endeavored to spike or destroy them by rolling them into the canal, and but for this precaution with the largest, the city would have been almost leveled to the dust.

No one slept during that night of horror, for added to the present scenes were the anticipations of what the morrow would bring forth. Daylight dawned upon a wreck of destruction and desolation. From the highest point of Church Hill and Libby Hill, the eye could range over the whole extent of city and country—the fire had not abated, and the burning bridges were adding their flame and smoke to the scene. A single faint explosion could be heard from the distance at long intervals, but the *Patrick Henry* was low to the water's edge and Drewry but a column of smoke. The whistle of the cars and the rushing of the laden trains still continued—they had never ceased—and the clouds hung low and draped the scene as morning advanced.

CHAPTER 17

"THERE WAS NO ASSIMILATION"
OF VICTORS AND VANQUISHED

BEFORE the sun had risen, two carriages rolled along Main Street, and passed through Rocketts just under Chimborazo Hospital, carrying the mayor and corporation towards the Federal lines, to deliver the keys of the city, and half an hour afterwards, over to the east, a single Federal blue-jacket rose above the hill, standing transfixed with astonishment at what he saw. Another and another sprang up as if out of the earth, but still all remained quiet. About seven o'clock, there fell upon the ear the steady clatter of horses' hoofs, and winding around Rocketts, close under Chimborazo Hill, came a small and compact body of Federal cavalrymen, on horses in splendid condition, riding closely and steadily along. They were well mounted, well accoutered, well fed—a rare sight in Southern streets,—the advance of that vaunted army that for four years had so hopelessly knocked at the gates of the Southern Confederacy.

They were some distance in advance of the infantry who followed, quite as well appointed and accoutered as the cavalry. Company after company, regiment after regiment, battalion after battalion, and brigade after brigade, they poured into the doomed city—an endless stream. One detachment separated from the main body and marching to Battery No. 2, raised the United States flag, their band playing the Star Spangled Banner. There they stacked their arms. The rest marched along Main Street through fire and smoke, over burning fragments of buildings, emerging at times like a phantom army when the wind lifted the dark clouds; while the colored population shouted and cheered them on their way.

Before three hours had elapsed, the troops had been quartered and were inspecting the city. They swarmed in every highway and byway, rose out of gullies, appeared on the top of hills, emerged from narrow lanes, and skirted around low fences. There was hardly a spot in Richmond not occupied by a blue coat, but they were orderly, quiet and respectful. Thoroughly disciplined, warned not to give offense by look or act, they did not speak to any one unless first addressed; and though the women of the South contrasted with sickness of heart the difference between this splendidly-equipped army, and the war-worn, wasted aspect of their own defenders, they were grateful for the consideration shown them; and if they remained in their sad homes, with closed doors and windows, or walked the streets with averted eyes and veiled faces, it was that they could not bear the presence of invaders, even under the most favorable circumstances.

Before the day was over, the public buildings were occupied by the enemy, and the minds of the citizens relieved from all fear of molestation. The hospitals were attended to, the ladies being still allowed to nurse and care for their own wounded; but rations could not be drawn yet, the obstructions in the James River preventing the transports from coming up to the city. In a few days they arrived, and food was issued to those in need.

It had been a matter of pride among the Southerners to boast that they had never seen a greenback, so the entrance of the Federal army had thus found them entirely unprepared with gold and silver currency. People who had boxes of Confederate money and were wealthy the day previously, looked around in vain for wherewithal to buy a loaf of bread. Strange exchanges were made on the street of tea and coffee, flour and bacon.

Those who were fortunate in having a stock of household necessaries were generous in the extreme to their less wealthy neighbors, but the destitution was terrible. The sanitary commission shops were opened, and commissioners appointed by the Federals to visit among the people and distribute orders to draw rations, but to effect this, after receiving tickets, required so many appeals to different officials, that decent people gave up the effort. Besides, the musty cornmeal and strong cod-fish were not appreciated by fastidious stomachs—few gently nurtured could relish such unfamiliar food.

But there was no assimilation between the invaders and invaded. In the daily newspaper a notice had appeared that the military bands would play in the beautiful capital grounds every afternoon, but when the appointed hour arrived, except the Federal officers, musicians and soldiers, not a white face was to be seen. The negroes crowded every bench and path.

The next week another notice was issued that the colored population would not be admitted; and then the absence of everything and anything feminine was appalling. The entertainers went alone to their own entertainment. The third week still another notice appeared: "colored nurses were to be admitted with their white charges," and lo! each fortunate white baby received the cherished care of a dozen finely-dressed black ladies, the only drawback being that in two or three days the music ceased altogether, the entertainers feeling at last the ingratitude of the subjugated people.

Despite their courtesy of manner, for however despotic the acts, the Federal authorities maintained a respectful manner—the newcomers made no advance towards fraternity. They spoke openly and warmly of their sympathy with the sufferings of the South, but committed and advocated acts that the hearers could not recognize as "military necessities." Bravely-dressed Federal officers met their former old class-mates from colleges and military institutions and inquired after the relatives to whose houses they had ever been welcome in days of yore, expressing a desire to "call and see them," while the vacant chairs, rendered vacant by Federal bullets, stood by the hearth of the widow and bereaved mother. They could not be made to understand that their presence was painful.

There were few men in the city at this time; but the women of the South still fought their battle for them: fought it resentfully, calmly, but silently! Clad in their mourning garments, overcome but hardly subdued, they sat within their desolate homes, or if compelled to leave that shelter went on their errands to church or hospital with veiled faces and swift steps. By no sign or act did the possessors of their fair city know that they were even conscious of their presence. If they looked in their faces they saw them not: they might have supposed themselves a phantom army. There was no stepping aside with affectation to avoid the contact of dress, no feigned humility in giving the inside of the walk: they simply totally ignored their presence.

Two particular characteristics followed the army in possession—the circus and booths for the temporary accommodation of itinerant venders. The small speculators must have supposed that there were no means of cooking left in the city, from the quantity of canned edibles they offered for sale. They inundated Richmond with pictorial canisters at exorbitant prices, which no one had money to buy. Whether the supply of greenbacks was scant, or the people were not disposed to trade with the newcomers, they had no customers.

In a few days steamboats had made their way to the wharves, though the obstructions still defied the ironclads, and crowds of curious strangers thronged the pavements, while squads of mounted male pleasure-seekers scoured the streets. Gayly-dressed women began to pour in also, with looped-up skirts, very large feet, and a great preponderance of spectacles. The Richmond women sitting by desolated firesides were astonished by the arrival of former friends, sometimes people moving in the best classes of society, who had the bad taste to make a pleasure trip to the mourning city, calling upon their heart-broken friends of happier days in all the finery of the newest New York fashions, and in some instances forgiving their entertainers the manifold sins of the last four years in formal and set terms.

From the hill on which my hospital was built, I had sat all the weary Sunday of the evacuation, watching the turmoil, and bidding friends adieu, for even till noon many had been unconscious of the events that were transpiring, and now when they had all departed, as night set in, I wrapped my blanket-shawl around me, and watched below me all that I have here narrated. Then I walked through my wards and found them comparatively empty. Every man who could crawl had tried to escape a Northern prison. Beds in which paralyzed, rheumatic, and helpless patients had laid for months were empty. The miracles of the New Testament had been re-enacted. The lame, the halt, and the blind had been cured.

Those who were compelled to remain were almost wild at being left in what would be the enemy's lines the next

day; for in many instances they had been exchanged prisoners only a short time before. I gave all the comfort I
could, and with some difficulty their supper also, for my
detailed nurses had gone with General Lee's army, and
my black cooks had deserted me.

On Monday morning, the day after the evacuation, the
first blue uniforms appeared at our quarters—three surgeons inspecting the hospital. As our surgeon was with
them, there must have been an amicable understanding.
One of our divisions was required for use by the newcomers, cleared out for them, and their patients laid by
the side of our own sick so that we shared with them, as
my own commissary stores were still well supplied. Three
days afterwards an order came to transfer my old patients
to Camp Jackson. I protested bitterly against this, as they
were not in a fit state for removal, so they remained
unmolested. To them I devoted my time, for our surgeons
had either then left or received orders to discontinue
their labors.

Towards evening the place was deserted. Miss G. had
remained up to this time with me, but her mother requiring her presence in the city, she left at sunset, and after I
had gone through all my wards, I returned to my dear
little sitting-room, endeared by retrospection, and the consciousness that my labors were nearly over, but had been
(as far as regarded results) in vain!

CHAPTER 18

"A WOMAN *MUST* SOAR BEYOND
THE CONVENTIONAL"

THE FEDERAL authorities had as yet posted no guards around, and as our own had been withdrawn, or rather had left, being under no control or direction, not a sound broke the stillness of the sad night. Exhausted with all the exciting events of the day, it was not to be wondered at that I soon fell asleep heavily and dreamlessly, to be awakened in an hour by the crash of an adjoining door, and passing into my pantry from whence the sound proceeded I came upon a group of men, who had burst the entrance opening upon the back premises.

As my eye traveled from face to face, I recognized them as a set of "hospital rats" whom I had never been able to get rid of, for if sent to the field one week, they would be sure to be back the next, on some trifling pretext of sickness or disability. The ringleader was an old enemy, who had stored up many a grievance against me, but my acts of kindness to his sickly wife naturally made me suppose his wrath had been disarmed. He acted on this occasion as spokesman, and the trouble was the old one. Thirty gallons of whiskey had been sent to me the day before the evacuation, and they wanted it.

"We have come for the whiskey!"

"You cannot, and shall not have it."

139

"It does not belong to you."

"It is in my charge, and I intend to keep it. Go out of my pantry; you are all drunk."

"Boys!" he said, "pick up that barrel and carry it down the hill. I will attend to *her!*"

But the habit of obedience of four years still had its effect on the boys, for all the movement they made was in a retrograde direction.

"Wilson," I said, "you have been in this hospital a long time. Do you think from what you know of me that the whiskey can be taken without my consent?"

He became very insolent.

"Stop that talk; your great friends have all gone, and we won't stand that now. Move out of the way!"

He advanced towards the barrel, and so did I, only being in the inside, I interposed between him and the object of contention. The fierce temper blazed up in his face, and catching me roughly by the shoulder, he called me a name that a decent woman seldom hears and even a wicked one resents.

But I had a little friend, which usually reposed quietly on the shelf, but had been removed to my pocket in the last twenty-four hours, more from a sense of protection than from any idea that it would be called into active service; so before he had time to push me one inch from my position, or to see what kind of an ally was in my hand, that sharp click, a sound so significant and so different from any other, struck upon his ear, and sent him back amidst his friends, pale and shaken.

"You had better leave," I said, composedly (for I felt in my feminine soul that although I was near enough to pinch his nose, that I had missed him), "for if *one* bullet is lost, there are five more ready, and the room is too small for even a woman to miss six times."

There was a conference held at the shattered door, resulting in an agreement to leave, but he shook his fist wrathfully at my small pop-gun.

"You think yourself very brave now, but wait an hour; perhaps others may have pistols too, and you won't have it entirely your way after all."

My first act was to take the head of one of the flour barrels and nail it across the door as tightly as I could, with a two-pound weight for a hammer, and then, warm with triumph and victory gained, I sat down by my whiskey barrel and felt the affection we all bestow on what we have cherished, fought for, and defended successfully; then putting a candle, a box of matches, and a pistol within reach of my hand, I went to sleep, never waking until late in the morning, having heard nothing more of my visitors.

The next day the steward informed me that our stores had been taken possession of by the Federal authorities, so we could not draw the necessary rations. The surgeons had all left; therefore I prepared for a visit to headquarters, by donning my full-dress toilette: boots of untanned leather, tied with thongs; a Georgia woven homespun dress in black and white blocks—the white, cotton yarn, the black, an old silk, washed, scraped with broken glass into pulp, and then carded and spun (it was an elegant thing); white cuffs and collar of bleached homespun, and a hat plaited of the rye straw picked from the field back of us, dyed black with walnut juice, a shoe-string for ribbon to encircle it; and knitted worsted gloves of three shades of green—the darkest bottle shade being around the wrist, while the color tapered to the loveliest blossom of the pea at the finger-tips. The style of the make was Confederate.

Thus splendidly equipped I walked to Dr. M.'s office, now Federal headquarters, and making my way through a crowd of blue coats, accosted the principal figure seated there, with a stern and warlike demand for food, and a curt inquiry whether it was their intention to starve their captured sick. He was very polite, laid the blame on the obstructions in the river, which prevented their transports getting up.

I requested that as such was the case I might be allowed to reclaim my ambulance, now under their lock and key, in order to take some coffee then in my possession to the city and exchange it for animal food. It had been saved from rations formerly drawn, and donations given. He wished to know why it had not been turned over to the U. S. government, but did not press the point as I was not communicative, and gave me the necessary order for the vehicle. Then polite conversation commenced.

"Was I a native of Virginia?"

"No; I was a South Carolinian, who had gone to Virginia at the commencement of the war to try and aid in alleviating the sufferings and privations of the hospitals."

"He had lost a brother in South Carolina."

"It was the fate of war. Self-preservation was the first law of nature. As a soldier he must recognize defense of one's native soil."

"He regretted the present state of scarcity, for he could see in the pale faces and pinched features of the Richmond women, how much they had suffered during the war."

I retorted quickly this wound to both patriotism and vanity.

He meant to be polite, but that he was unlucky was shown by my answer.

"If my features were pinched, and my face pale, it was not caused by privations under the Confederacy, but the anguish consequent upon our failure."

But his kindness had once again put my ambulance under my control, and placing a bag of coffee and a demijohn of whiskey in it, I assumed the reins, having no driver, and went to market. The expedition was successful, as I returned shortly with a live calf, for which I had exchanged them, and which summoned every one within hearing by its bellowing. I had quite won the heart of the Vermonter who had been sentry at my door, and though patriotic souls may not believe me, he paid me many compliments at the expense of the granite ladies of his state. The compliments were sincere, as he refused the drink of whiskey my gratitude offered him.

My next visit was to the commissary department of my hospital in search of sugar. Two Federal guards were in charge, but they simply stared with astonishment as I put aside their bayonets and unlocked the door of the place with my pass-key, filled my basket, with an explanation to them that I could be arrested whenever wanted at my quarters.

After this no one opposed my erratic movements, the newcomers ignoring me. No explanation was ever given to me, why I was allowed to come and go, nurse my men and feed them with all I could take or steal. All I ever gathered was from one of our errand-boys, who had fraternized with a Yankee sutler, who told him confidentially that the Federal surgeon in charge thought that woman in black had better go home, and added on his own responsibility, "He's awful afraid of her."

Away I was compelled to go at last, for my sick were
removed to another hospital, where I still attended to
them. There congregated the ladies of the neighborhood,
bringing what delicacies they could gather, and nursing
indiscriminately any patient who needed care. This continued till all the sick were either convalescent or dead,
and at last my vocation was gone, and not one invalid
left to give me a pretext for daily occupation.

And now when the absorbing duties of the last years
no longer demanded my whole thoughts and attention,
the difficulties of my own position forced themselves upon
my mind. Whatever food had been provided for the sick
since the Federal occupation had served for my small
needs, but when my duties ceased I found myself with a
box full of Confederate money and a silver ten-cent piece;
perhaps a Confederate *gage d'amitie;* which puzzled me
how to expend. It was all I had for a support, so I bought
a box of matches and five cocoa-nut cakes. The wisdom
of the purchase there is no need of defending. Should
any one ever be in a strange country where the currency
of which he is possessed is valueless, and ten cents be his
only available funds, perhaps he may be able to judge
of the difficulty of expending it with judgment.

But of what importance was the fact that I was house-
less, homeless and moneyless, in Richmond, the heart of
Virginia? Who ever wanted for aught that kind hearts,
generous hands or noble hospitality could supply, that it
was not there offered without even the shadow of a
patronage that could have made it distasteful? What
women were ever so refined in feeling and so unaffected
in manner; so willing to share all that wealth gives, and
so little infected with the pride of purse that bestows that
power? It was difficult to hide one's needs from them;
they found them out and ministered to them with their

quiet simplicity and the innate nobility which gave to their generosity the coloring of a favor received; not conferred.

I laughed carelessly and openly at the disregard shown by myself for the future, when every one who had remained in Richmond, apparently had laid aside stores for daily food, but they detected with quick sympathy the hollowness of the mirth, and each day at every hour of breakfast, dinner and supper, would come to me a waiter, borne by the neat little Virginia maid (in her white apron), filled with ten times the quantity of food I could consume, packed carefully on. Sometimes boxes would be left at my door, with packages of tea, coffee, sugar and ham, or chicken, and no clue given to the thoughtful and kind donor.

Would that I could do more than thank the dear friends who made my life for four years so happy and contented; who never made me feel by word or act, that my self-imposed occupation was otherwise than one which would ennoble any woman. If ever any aid was given through my own exertions, or any labor rendered effective by me for the good of the South—if any sick soldier ever benefited by my happy face or pleasant smiles at his bedside, or death was ever soothed by gentle words of hope and tender care, such results were only owing to the cheering encouragement I received from them. They were gentlewomen in every sense of the word, and though they might not have remembered that *"noblesse oblige"* they felt and acted up to the motto in every act of their lives. My only wish was to live and die among them, growing each day better from contact with their gentle, kindly sympathies and heroic hearts.

It may never be in my power to do more than offer my heartfelt thanks, which may reach their once happy homes;

and in closing these simple reminiscences of hospital experience, let me beg them to believe that whatever kindness my limited powers have conferred on the noble soldiers of their state, has been repaid tenfold, leaving with me an eternal, but grateful obligation.

*　　*　　*　　*　　*　　*

There is one subject connected with hospitals on which a few words should be said—the distasteful one that a woman must lose a certain amount of delicacy and reticence in filling any office in them. How can this be? There is no unpleasant exposure under proper arrangements, and if even there be, the circumstances which surround a wounded man, far from friends and home, suffering in a holy cause and dependent upon a woman for help, care and sympathy, hallow and clear the atmosphere in which she labors. That woman must indeed be hard and gross, who lets one material thought lessen her efficiency. In the midst of suffering and death, hoping with those almost beyond hope in this world; praying by the bedside of the lonely and heart-stricken; closing the eyes of boys hardly old enough to realize man's sorrows, much less suffer by man's fierce hate, a woman *must* soar beyond the conventional modesty considered correct under different circumstances.

If the ordeal does not chasten and purify her nature, if the contemplation of suffering and endurance does not make her wiser and better, and if the daily fire through which she passes does not draw from her nature the sweet fragrance of benevolence, charity, and love,—then, indeed a hospital has been no fit place for her!

Letters From Wartime Richmond

CHAPTER 19

"MRS. JEFF IS GROWING VERY FINE"

Marietta, 29 November, 1862

I have been waiting to write you, dear sister E.[1], till I could tell you where to direct to me, and only received a letter today giving me information that will direct my future movements. I leave here next Wednesday or Thursday to take charge of one of the Hospitals at Richmond.

You know how unpleasantly I have been situated at Papa's house, and owing to his indifference, I see no chance of bettering my position while there,—one child takes pattern after the other, and any little difference or conflict of opinions results in a desire that they may never have to live with me, or be with me, or something of the kind. I hope that Mrs. Anzi will have told Brother[2] some of the occurrences that took place here this summer. I was loath to go away under the false accusations made against me, for I felt the force of the old proverb, "Give a dog a bad name." Mrs. Nott and Mrs. Anzi heard all that went on with their own ears and saw with their own eyes and so did all the house here,—they were as kind and sympathizing as if they were my own family. I can never forget Mrs. Anzi's affectionate kindness.

You may imagine how frightened and nervous I feel concerning the step I am about to take and how important in its small way it will be to me, for I have too much

1. Eugenia (Mrs. Philip) Phillips.
2. Samuel Yates Levy.

149

common sense to underrate what I am giving up. I care more for the worldly interests [?] I give up, than the labors I take upon myself, but I have had such kind friends that it makes me brave, and I look forward with pleasure to any life that will exempt me from daily jealousies and rudenesses. I shall speak to Papa today and really believe that the step I take will be a relief to him.

I have not thanked you for my gloves; they were a great acquisition and are the only pair of any kind that I have had for ten months. How could you come out of New Orleans without some black cloathes [*sic.*] for me? I would pay any price for any of the necessary things for mourning. Do if you have anything in the way of shoes, boots or gloves, or anything at all not wanted let me buy it, it will be the greatest favor that can be done me, nothing could come amiss. You may think how badly off I am when I am having a petticoat quilted of an old gingham dress, and Mrs. Gen. Lovell[3] and Nancy are sitting in my room finishing off my dresses made of common home spun for which I gave one dollar a yard, to wear in the place of flannel.

I hope that you will write to me and cheer me up, for I have not the most enlivening life before me, and if I have time to answer letters they will be my chiefest pleasure. I hear a great deal of Richmond gossip—and that it is a very scandalizing place for gay and fashionable women. Mrs. Joe Johnson[4] is quite a leader of tea, and Mrs. McLane, Gen. Sumner's daughter, is the chere ami of Mrs. Jeff. Davis. Mrs. McL. was suspected of being a spy and sent on to Richmond under surveillance, but very private, as her husband stands high in the army, and when around

---

3. Probably Mrs. Mansfield Lovell, whose husband was in command at New Orleans before the Federals occupied that city.
4. Mrs. Joseph E. Johnston, nee Lydia McLane of Maryland.

there Mrs. Greenhow was paid to watch her.[5] They make a very amusing story of it, however, for the report says that Lincoln pays Mrs. McLane for her information and Jeff. Davis pays Mrs. Greenhow for watching her, and Mrs. G. is also paid by the Federals for not seeing too much and lastly that the two ladies are in collusion and divide the spoils.

I have not told you of my pecuniary affairs. I am to have board and lodging in the Hospital and at a boarding house adjacent and forty dollars a month, which will clothe me. I have entire charge of my department, seeing that everything is cleanly, orderly and all prescriptions of physicians given in proper time, food properly prepared and so on. I had the choice of the large Hospital at Cotoosa Springs, formerly the Hotel under Dr. Foster, the Chimborazo Hospital at Richmond, or one at Atlanta, and chose the Richmond one, because it was divided among half a dozen ladies who would be companionable perhaps. Cotoosa is very bleak and lonely & I have no warm clothing, besides Dr. Foster is a friend, very pleasant, handsome and intelligent, and as we would be comparatively alone and eat together, *that* would not do. Tell Fanny[6] that she has never remembered me in any of her letters, give her my love, also to your husband. I am sorry that I did not see Brother while he was here, except for a moment in Mrs. Anzi's room. I don't wonder that you feel attached to people so kind as those you are among. I am writing in great haste. I have just finished a letter to Mrs. Randolph accepting the place of matron and want to get both of them in the mail.

---

5. Mrs. Rose O'Neal Greenhow was a famous spy for the Confederacy. Mrs. McLane, daughter of General E. V. Sumner, was a favorite in Richmond war-time society. Mary Boykin Chesnut, in one of several references to her in *A Diary from Dixie* states (June 27, 1861): "Mrs. McLane is here. Mrs. Davis always has clever women around her."
6. Phoebe's niece, daughter of Mrs. Philip Phillips.

Anything in the way of clothing that you do not need please let me have. I will thankfully pay double, and feel no delicacy I have plenty of money, but no effects. If you prefer silver I will exchange with you. I was going to beg for my Balmoral back again, but John told me it was defunct. Should the fate of war take me to Washington, I shall join my fate to Elsie's. Please answer my letter here; I may not go as soon as I think. My duties commence the 1 December. Anyway I shall leave word to have my letters forwarded to Richmond.

With a great deal of love and hopes that we may meet again & that you will believe that nothing but the strongest pressure could force me out into the world in such a painful and laborious life, believe me affectionately yours,

                                                        Phebe

                        Richmond, Vir. 30 Jan. 1863

I received the chemise russe, dear Sister E., for which receive my thanks. The missing sleeve was replaced by a piece of my shawl which I preferred cutting up, as there was no black merino in Richmond. I cannot add to my other obligations by letting you pay the express, small as that sum is compared to the value of the body, [?] so enclose the money, you know a person must begin to pay somewhere and I may as well commence here. It fit beautifully and looks nicely with a homespun skirt I got from North Carolina.

I wrote a note to Henrietta Lay asking the questions you wanted answered, and forgot to send it—however I gave it to Col. Gilmer yesterday to hand to Judge Campbell who is in the War Department where he goes every day,

and will enclose her answer.[7] I can give you some little
information myself which is reliable, as I got it from the
lips of Mrs. Swan of Baltimore who has just come over in
the flag of truce boat from Washington. Sally Carroll
married Griffin of the Army—her brother was killed in
one of the battles before Richmond. Old Gaultier, dis-
gusted with the black Republican government, has shut
up shop and gone to live in Paris—the Rev. Mr. Elliott,
I think, an Episcopal minister in Washington, prayed for
Jeff. Davis openly in church on Christmas day, and these
are the only items I remember at present.

Poor Mrs. Lay seems to have made an unfortunate
match both as to character and position. I hear the officers
laughing very much at Lay, who appears to be a good
natured butt, hardly ever sober. He holds no commission
since Virginia turned over her troops to the Confederate
government & they say wrote a very good article on the
defences of Mobile which nobody wanted, and which
if needed would have been meritorious.

Of the fashionable world I can tell you nothing. I am
living out at Chimborazo Hospital in a whitewashed
board house through the planks of which I can see the
stars and the snow too. It is divided into three parts:
the first my parlor and chamber in one. The second my
kitchen and the third my Laundry. I am sitting all alone
writing, for everybody but the sick soldiers and the nurses
have gone away, and the nearest house to me is fifty yards
off. I have little sliding windows like the cabin of a ship,
and when it rains I put my straw mattress in the center of
my room as it comes through the planks. At all hours of
the day and night you can see me around the wards with

7. Jeremy F. Gilmer, Chief Engineer of the Confederate Army, was pro-
moted major general Aug. 25, 1863. John A. Campbell, of Alabama, Associate
Justice of the U. S. Supreme Court, 1853-1861, was during the Civil War
Assistant Secretary of War in the Confederacy.

my greatest treasure: Miss Amanda's shawl over my head and a bowl or cup in my hand, and I never see a human being but the sick. Each man either receives what is needed if not from my hands from under my eyes, and nourished by it gets well or dies with the consciousness that there is someone by his pillow that is doing all that can be done. Towards evening my duties are lighter, and I take a little rest but at night I either write for the magazines or copy writing for the Department, as Congress made a ridiculous appropriation for the matrons, only forty dollars a month and fifteen for commutation, making fifty-five dollars and washing is over three dollars a dozen and every expense in proportion. I wrote out a memorial for increase in pay and sent it to my friend old Foote who I knew would be glad of any opportunity to hear himself talk on any subject. However I am perfectly happy, have more than sufficient [means] for my small wants, and thrown upon myself for occupation attend more thoroughly to my duties than I possibly could under other circumstances.

Sometimes a stray visitor comes out to see the "Hospital on the Hill" as was the case of Mrs. Garnett of Washington. She told me that Mrs. Mallory had been very anxious to know of my whereabouts and begged me to send her my card.[8] My assistant matron Miss Ball went to Mrs. Jeff.[9] to get a place in the Treasury note signing room for her sister, and Mrs. Jeff. who is growing very fine said that "places were hard to get, some of the first ladies in the country had applied for the position of housekeeper to her among them Judge Berman's daughter, Mrs. Barton, but said Mrs. Jeff. how could I give it to her—the President could not sit at table with my house-

8. Mrs. Stephen F. Mallory, wife of the Confederate Secretary of Navy.
9. Mrs. Jefferson Davis.

keeper." I go to town to buy delicacies for my sick very often, in my own ambulance, which I call my Volante from some distinction of ideas and the black boy who drives me, "Miss Hensler's Avalanch." I met Benjamin and Lt. Martin but they did not recognize me, as I was holding the reins and bargaining for apples which by the by are three for a dollar. If you want any letters sent to the North I have no difficulty in getting them there, as some one goes every week. Mrs. Lawton whose husband was shot at Fredericksburg went to him through a pass from Gen. Burnside. She was received by Gen. Sumner and treated most kindly, found the body of her husband embalmed, and his watch and valuables safely deposited waiting for her. The ladies (southern) of Alexandria were devoted to her. Thinking she had no Federal money they sent her all her mourning from her shoes to her crape veil. She staid at Col. Gilmer's house on her return with her husband's body, and we had a sad time. He was a young man of great promise.

I was very sorry that the silk dress was unfit to send for the poor girl's sake who needed it. She is the Miss Ball I have before spoken of, perhaps you remember the constant mention after the battle of Manassas of the burning of the Ball house. I have no means of disposing of such elegant dresses as you name, although from what I hear they would bring fabulous prices in Richmond. You might send me the lace; perhaps I could sell that, or any collars or sleeves you have.

I hear very often from Mrs. Anzi, and she rather puzzled me in her last letter when she said that Col. Phillips[10] "was much gratified at the successful issue of his wife's visit to Marietta in making peace all round." I don't know

---

10. Philip Phillips, Phoebe's brother-in-law. The title apparently was honorary.

what *that* means, and so I told her. Adele also wrote me quite an affectionate letter, and I was much surprised by one from Mrs. Lovell telling me that Mrs. George Walker[11]—(Gen. Walker's wife) felt some delicacy in offering her services on a short acquaintance but if I preferred to sign Treasury notes, she could easily get me an appointment. Indeed every day brings me some remembrance from people I hardly knew or spoke to last summer, and though I notice you slur upon my pleasant manners taking strangers, believe me the world is not easily gulled and seldom if their preference is founded upon a person's manners, cares about them when away from their influence.

I had to stop here to go to one of my patients who sent to me to come and see if he was dying and poor fellow he could only ask the question before he died. I sometimes wonder if I am the same person who was afraid to look at a dead person, for I have no timidity and hardly any sensibility left. I closed the poor fellow's eyes, took his name and money and here I am again, all alone, never thinking of anything but for comfort of the living. After the battle of Fredericksburg I stood by and saw men's fingers and arms cut off and held the brandy to their lips, washing the wounds myself. It is amusing to see their heads pop from under their clothing in bed the moment they hear my name in the morning like turtles out of the shell, and still more amusing to hear their wants as I go round with my slate, not only do they say what they need, but how they wish me to cook it. Some of their receipts are most atrocious, and only this morning I asked a man if he wanted the mixture of bread, milk, pepper and salt to put upon his chest, or to eat.

---

11. Possibly the wife of Maj. Gen. John G. Walker of Missouri. Mrs. Lovell was the wife of Gen. Mansfield Lovell, who had been in command at New Orleans before the fall of that city.

I saw Mrs. Hopkins[12] a week ago—I went to the Alabama Hospital to ask her where she boarded if I could
get a room, living out at Chimborazo was so dull—she was
full however of herself and her duties and I did not stay
long. Board here is a hundred dollars a month, but when
I told the surgeon general that I wanted to take the Crenshaw Hospital, not liking my present position he said that
I might board anywhere, gave me an ambulance but said
I must not leave him—so I suppose my services are valuable. However I cannot in conscience let him pay one
hundred dollars for my board when my pay is only forty.
I staid nearly two months at Col. Gilmer's where they had
a very pleasant mess, but he will not let me bear my share
of the expenses. I was almost afraid to ask him what I
owed him with tea at twelve dollars a pound and coffee
at five.

I received a letter from Fanny, and have tried hard to
embroider a baby shirt for Lena but it is an impossibility,
for I have not only to be going all the time, but my hands
are full. I have not been able to get a cook and everything
for seven hundred sick men has to be cooked under my
eyes by two black imps of fourteen—as you may suppose
my hands are never clean—and I get so weary I cannot
sew.

What can I tell you interesting? I hear very often from
sister and her family but you are not interested in what
goes on there and with an immense correspondence it is
with people you do not care about or know. The only
book I have read has been Bulwer's strange story, and if
he had called it a stupid story he would have been nearer
the mark. I think your picture of rural life very taking

12. Mrs. Arthur F. Hopkins, Confederate nurse, who pioneered the organization of the Alabama unit at Chimborazo and who was wounded at Seven
Pines. She and her husband are said to have contributed $200,000 for the care
of the sick, wounded and needy.

for those who like it, but I prefer where I am and what I am doing, what good that is I leave report to tell you, and I thank God every night for the courage He gave me to leave those who never cared for me and I believe disliked me for the gifts He had given me. I bring comfort, strength and I believe happiness to many sick beds daily and lie down at night with a happy consciousness of time well and unselfishly spent—if as I was told the children of these men will "rise up and call me blessed" I shall have many blessings. Do give my love . . . [part of letter missing].

CHAPTER 20

"AMONG FEVER WARDS AND DYING MEN"

Richmond. 25 June. 1863.

Dear sister E,

Eugene[1] brought me your letter in person—which tho' very pleasant was not half as agreeable as it ought to have been considering how long it took to get it up—you are not like Edward Everett who having taken fourteen years to write his memorial of Washington produced at last a masterpiece. But I am not in any way detracting from the pleasure its receipt gave me.

Eugene has altered very little, except he has become a great talker, a talent I really believe lying dormant in all the family ready to bloom at any moment. His vessel lies about fourteen miles from Richmond, opposite Drewey's Bluff and when he comes to the city, he is compelled to land just under Chimborazo Hill. I told him as I tell you that anything that lies in my power to make him comfortable, or to add to his pleasure, I will do willingly. He seems to be very happy and comfortable and I see no chance of any temptations being presented to him situated where he is. He brought a young friend the last time he came here, a "Texican" as one of my ward nurses called him, a very nice, gentle quiet young fellow who I think will just do for him. When you write to Eugene tell him

---

1. Eugene Phillips, son of Philip Phillips, and nephew of Phoebe Pember. He was a Confederate Naval Cadet, on the *Patrick Henry,* a training vessel anchored on the James River below Richmond. See E. M. Coulter, *The Confederate States of America* (Baton Rouge, 1950), 299.

whenever he wants to spend a day in town to come to me, and if it will be allowed on ship, I can always give him a bed as I have two rooms, one at the Hospital and one in town.

We are still having most delightful weather sleeping with closed windows and under a blanket and tho' I dreaded the summer very much I think I can easily bear three months of heat counting from the first of July. The walk to and from the Hospital is rather appalling in very warm weather as there is no shade, only a long but sandy stretch, but it will not be for very long as when the fall comes I shall again stay in my shanty.

I have nothing of interest to tell you, as I have been in bed for the last two weeks with rheumatizm and have seen very few people, the Richmonders are going rural at this season paying visits to the neighboring plantations and many of them have been caught by the raiders who are now only ten miles from the city. The public attention is fixed upon Gen. Lee who having got Hooker away from Fredericksburg and in the vicinity of Alexandria, just where he wants him to be—will have to whip him before he advances into Pennsylvania, as it will be impossible to leave such an army in his rear. Whatever Lee's plans are he has managed to keep his own counsel as even the military men in the highest posts are unacquainted with them. However Mrs. Davis gives out and is aided and abetted in her announcement by all the ignorant ones that Lee has not moved from Culpeper. Mrs. Long, the wife of Col. Long of the Confederate Army and daughter of Gen. Sumner, has just returned from New York.[2] She was to have brought me all I needed, but it has been a great disappointment. Lincoln gave her a pass (as she

2. Mrs. Armistead L. Long, whose husband was on Lee's staff, was the daughter of Federal General E. V. Sumner. When after the war Long lost his sight, President Grant appointed Mrs. Long Postmistress of Charlottesville, Va.

went to him herself) allowing her to bring everything she had, but in stepping into the cars at Baltimore she was arrested by order of Gen. Fish who opened her trunks and only let her take out certain articles. For instance two, out of a dozen boxes, of black pins, one shawl out of five and three pairs of gloves out of a dozen. With quite a refinement of cruelty he only let her bring heavy winter clothing, knowing she was coming to a very warm climate. Mrs. McLean and herself came yesterday to tell me the cheerful news and to give me all she had—a couple of lemmons. Mrs. McLean[3] is still staying with Mrs. Davis. If you think it will ever be in your power to buy me anything in black I will send you a draft, things are cheaper anywhere than in Richmond. I paid sixty five dollars for a black barege! Anything in black will be of service either as a dress or petticoat and Confederate money is not worth keeping. Tell me if I shall send you some money and wait my chance? You need not feel any hesitation in letting me do so, for I have more than I need and I make it very quickly and very easily. I wish that I could take advantage of your offer to let Phebe help me in my sewing as I have to give out everything not having a moment's spare time, but the express bill would amount to quite as much as the work paid for here. I have laughed as you did at the report concerning the large fortune I ignored, but I heard it in another way, that I "had refused a large fortune" from such patriotic views—and—who knows I *may* perhaps one of these days have a chance of doing so if any one with a large fortune proposes.

I had quite a party here just before I was sick—some of the prettiest girls in Richmond—The Cary's, Hettie and Constance, Mary Garnett, Misses Marye, Harrison,

---

3. Probably a misspelling of Mrs. McLane, General Sumner's daughter, sister of Mrs. Armistead L. Long. See Mary B. Chesnut, *A Diary from Dixie,* 89.

Robinson, Saunders, all beauties.[4] They were matronized by Mrs. Gen. Myers, who has turned up again into fashionable life with a five week old baby.[5] They all came at six o'clock, eat strawberries and ice cream, walked all around the Bluff and at eleven were driven home by their respective cavaliers. The next evening we all went down to Drewry's Bluff in a government boat and visited the fortifications & the gunboats. I suppose that you are surprised at my seeing so much company, but if I did not make an effort to be agreeable and encourage people to come to me I should be very isolated and lonely. The Haxalls[6] and Mrs. Allen call for me to drive very often. Mrs. Allen was an old acquaintance, Pick Hoffman from Baltimore.

Mrs. Long gave me a great deal of news from the North. She staid at the Latrobe's and says the spirit is still indomitable among the Baltimore women. Their last fashion was to wear cents as brooches, which as soon as the Federals found meant "Copperheads" they were arrested. Photographs of Jackson were selling all over the city, till the gallery which issued them was shut up by military order and the last taken sold for three hundred dollars apiece. After his death everyone who wore black was arrested. There is nothing very new in the fashions—a shirt point in front and a little jacket tail behind with three buttons. Dresses very high with a standing bias piece of silk with a *very* narrow little frill in lace at the top in place of ribbon

---

4. The "girls" referred to were favorites in the society of Confederate Richmond. They moved in the same circles as Mrs. Chesnut and some of them are mentioned repeatedly in *A Diary from Dixie* and in DeLeon's *Belles, Beaux and Brains of the 60's.*

5. Wife of Quartermaster General A. C. Myers, a belle whose reference at a dinner party to Mrs. Jefferson Davis as "an old squaw," according to Richmond gossip, contributed to Myers' supersedure by Gen. A. R. Lawton.

6. The Haxalls were described by DeLeon in *Belles, Beaux and Brains of the 60's,* p. 126, as "one of the most noted families in recent Richmond and one that took on biblical proportions."

and collar. And to make up for so little white, an immense white muslin bow with rumeled[?] ends trimmed with deep lace. The hair instead of drooping is worn very high, with all sorts of things in the top. Mrs. Long declares sometimes a bird's with the setting mother. She also described a novelty in the shape of a serpent winding around the head with the crest over the left ear—this is an India rubber tube and in entering the screw is turned and the lady throws out a brilliant jet of flame which lasts fifteen minutes. The idea taken from the Empress going to a fancy ball as a volcano. The most curious article I have seen lately is a small trumpet that hangs to the watch chain inside there is a glass about as large as the head of a big pin with nine little specks—in looking through the end you distinctly see the perfect portraits of our nine generals! The Baltimore ladies wear them. Five were brought here for sale and I sent for one I wished to give sister, but I was too sick to go myself and am very much afraid I won't get it.

I hear very often from all my friends—they are scattered in every direction—Mrs. Maury at Shelbyville— Mrs. Caskill at Winchester, Mrs. Soule at Columbus and Mrs. Yandell at Cartersville.[7] Mrs. Anzi tells me that Brother is in Mobile and passed the evening with them. Col. Pickett[8] came out to invite me to go to the natural bridge with him, but I would not put myself under the pecuniary obligation. Dr. McCaw, the surgeon in chief of Hospitals sent me word that I had overworked myself and required change, giving me a furlough for six weeks, but I declined taking advantage of it not having any

7. None of these women can be positively identified. Possibly Mrs. Maury was the wife of General Dabney H. Maury and Mrs. Yandell of David W. Yandell, Chief Surgeon, Army of Tennessee.

8. Possibly Col. John T. Pickett, Confederate commissioner to Mexico and chief of staff to Gen. John C. Breckinridge.

place I cared to go to, nor anything nice to wear. Since then
I received a warm invitation from my friend Mrs. McBlair
who is living at Charlotte, N. C., and may go there next
month. Tell Fan[9] with my love that I have none but Georgians in my Hospital though a gentleman from N. C. did
come here without a furlough for love of "mes beaus
yeux." What does she mean by saying that Fanny[10] would
hardly trifle with Walsh, he was such an *"unfortunate
young man."* I wish that Fanny would come up during the
fall and spend a couple of months with me. If she would
come as my assistant I could send her a transportation
ticket. All the girls here are in the different departments
they make a frolic of it. Give my love and congratulations
to Lena.[11] I have a little shirt half embroidered that I
could not finish that I shall have to keep for Fanny. What
has Lena called her baby? Give my kindest love to Mrs.
Amanda and remembrance to all.

Truly yours

Phebe

Richmond. 13 September. 1863.

As I am confined to my room, my dear sister, I think
that I had better fill up the leisure time by answering my
letters, and yours comes first upon the list. I have been
quite sick with no actual disease but only what the English
call "a low state." I think that during the intense summer
heats, being so much in the gangrenous and Typhus
wards, that the infected air may have induced this state
—with all the precautions of cleanliness and ventilation

---

9. Daughter of Mrs. Philip Phillips.
10. Fanny Cohen, daughter of Phoebe's sister, Henrietta. Fanny Cohen in
1867 married Henry Taylor of Savannah.
11. Lena is Caroline Phillips (Mrs. Fred) Myers, to whom a daughter,
Eugenia, recently had been born.

the air will become close when each bed is only allowed a certain number of feet. Dr. McCaw sent me a furlough but I had no where to go, for if even I had the means to pay the enormous board charged I could not go alone. I am all right again, I believe, for the cool weather has set in. Our surgeon Dr. Habersham went off and so did my assistant, Miss Ball, so that double work fell on me. I suggested to the surgeon in chief to make me surgeon in charge, on the ground that Toney Lumpkin's mother had been a Colonel and his Aunt, a justice of the peace, but nothing came of it.

I have not seen Eugene for some time, but heard that they were all studying very hard. I met him on Main Street looking very nicely in his undress uniform, which I believe he removed all Creation to get. I would not give him too much money if I were you. He gets more than enough to support himself, fifty dollars a month, ten of which goes to his mess bill. All his clothing he gets at government price and I have his washing done for him. They charge three dollars a dozen here and as I am entitled to have mine done at one dollar at the Hospital, I extend the permission to his. This leaves him fifty dollars a month clear, quite enough for a boy of his age. It is all that *I* get and I make it answer, though I pay full price for all wearing apparel. I have told him to come to me for all the sewing and mending he wants done, and you need not tell him anything on the subject, as if I object to do what he might ask, I should have no delicacy in telling him so.

I am more than surprised at the desponding tone of your letters—you ought to be with the Army and hear the soldiers talk—I would like anybody to tell *them* that they had been beaten at Gettysburg, or anywhere else, they will laugh in your face. They have been obliged, they allow, to

fall back before superior forces at times, but never where
there have been any equality of numbers. I have never had
a doubt of the final end, even if, as you say "LaGrange
should become a frontier town." I live almost in the Army
and find every man willing to fight to the end—they are
patient, enduring and brave and such material cannot fail.
There has been a cabinet of war sitting at the President's
for the last week, resulting in Gen. Lee being sent with a
large part of the Army to Tennessee. Meade, they say,
has but *one* effective corps and Pickett's division can keep
that in check here. I went to town to pay a visit at the
Warwick's and a gentleman stopping to hand me out of
an awkward ambulance proved to be Gen. Lee. He looked
much older and greatly worn.

I shall lose very kind and devoted friends by Davis
appointing Gilmer a Major General, and sending him to
Charleston. I have spent every evening with them for five
months, and shall have no place to go now. I live a mile
and a half from the city proper. As a sett off Mrs. Lawton
has come in as Lawton has been made Quarter Master
General, but she lives where all my other friends live, at
the extreme West End, it makes the prospect of the coming winter very gloomy for me, for though I have an
ambulance it is against orders for it to leave the Hospital
after eight o'clock which precludes all spending the evening out. Gen. Gilmer writes very hopefully from Charleston, he says that the enemy will certainly take Sumter.
Gregg. Moultrie and Simpkins, as they have already taken
Wagner; but the inner line of defenses is very strong,
time is of the greatest importance, to strengthen the city,
as the call of Beauregard for negroes to work had not been
properly complied with. Beauregard seems to have got a
little above himself and transmitted all his orders thro'
Jordan, a man who was, or rather had made himself, so

obnoxious to the citizens that they paid no attention to his demands.[12] I hear from what the newspapers say is reliable authority, that at the time of the first attack Ripley[13] and Jordan were so engaged in blockade running that the safety of their expected cargoes were uppermost in their minds, instead of the safety of the city. Ripley has made a million they say and Jordan half as much. Gen. Gilmer counts a great deal upon the high equinoctial winds at this season among the clumsy and unmanageable Monitors and also upon those three iron clad steamers now receiving their armament in France. The splendid guns, firing six hundred and seventy five pounds, have been mounted in the battery in the city, and also a morter throwing a shell weighing four hundred and twenty five pounds. Gen. Gilmer pronounced all the defenses at Savannah and in the harbor useless as they were constructed with mud, through which the new projectiles go without difficulty—they are cutting them down and building them of sand, he thinks in time.

I wish that Fanny would accept Kate Campbell's invitation and come for a time to Richmond.[14] I would give her half my room with pleasure, whenever she would come to me, and it is quite as nice as at any hotel, it is away from the Hospital to which she need not come unless she wished to do so, and even then my office, parlor, kitchen and laundry are pretty far from the wards, with which she would not be brought into contact. I have a sweetheart for her, though I am not much of a match maker, he is a nephew of Gen. Lee one of the Shirley

12. The reference is to Col. Thomas Jordan, Beauregard's chief of staff.
13. Gen. R. S. Ripley, who earlier had been in command at Charleston, was at this time subordinate to Gen. P. G. T. Beauregard and at odds with both Beauregard and Jordan. The report about blockade running apparently was one of the many wild rumors to which the Confederacy was subjected.
14. The Fanny here mentioned was Fanny Phillips, Phoebe's niece, who later married Charles Hill. Kate Campbell was the daughter of Assistant Secretary of War John A. Campbell.

Carters of Brentford, the oldest Virginia family extant
that is also his name and a sweet fellow he is, about
twenty six. I have talked to him (for he comes to see me
almost daily) about Fanny till he is half in love with her,
and I think he could win any girl's heart. Ask Lena if she
will not give me Fanny's Daguerreotype I gave her last
winter. I hope that she will not refuse me such a trifle,
particularly as she was indebted to my generosity for it.

The feeling here against the Yankees exceeds anything
I could imagine, particularly among the good Christians.
I spent an evening among a particularly pious sett. One
lady said she had a pile of Yankee bones lying around
her pump so that the first glance on opening her eyes
would rest upon them. Another begged me to get her a
Yankee Skull to keep her toilette trinkets in. All had
something of the kind to say—at last I lifted my voice
and congratulated myself at being born of a nation, and
religion that did not enjoin forgiveness on its enemies,
that enjoyed the blessed privilege of praying for an eye
for an eye, and a life for a life, and was not one of those
for whom Christ died in vain, considering the present
state of feeling. I proposed that till the war was over they
should all join the Jewish Church, let forgiveness and
peace and good will alone and put their trust in the
sword of the Lord and Gideon. It was a very agreeable
evening, and all was taken in good part. I certainly had
the best of the argument, and the gentlemen seconded me
ably. Yesterday some of the gentlemen came out, among
them Major Coxe, who asked me after either you or the
girls, he is a very fine looking, rather dissipated looking
man.

I paid a visit yesterday about which I would like to
consult you, not about the visit but the results, as you are
acquainted with one of the parties—the friend I called

on spoke very kindly of the life of exertion and self-sacrifice she fancied I was leading, dilated very strongly upon the sinfulness and scandal making of any woman who would or could say anything reflecting upon me— and to make a long story short I found that Mrs. L-y was the mischief maker. She brought no charges it seems against me only that small and mean style of *surmising* which is worse than damning with faint praise. *"She* knew what brought me to Richmond, no one could tell *her* anything about *me*—if I lived alone I had my reasons" —all this is very bad and very malicious, my life is irreproachable now as it morally always has been; there is nothing in the past or the present to touch it; my time is past from morning till night by the bedside of the sick and dying, fulfilling to the extent of my capability the duties of my position, never considering my personal comfort, living what to most women would be a life of self abnegation and sacrifice, but which is neither to me. Every one I come in contact with has respected and made much of me and here comes this woman pretending to know something wrong in my former life and present motives. It is like a small but poisonous sting. Would you advise me to see her and speak to her of the mischief she does, or not to notice the matter? You know my life is a little peculiar. I am entirely independent and alone, per-haps younger and more attractive than the very old and very unattractive women who fill these positions and the world might put any construction upon the matter they pleased. She said that she had heard from my sister that my work was entirely a matter of choice, but I immediately contradicted this (as the choice of such a life would naturally be considered an absurdity) and said I had no means and it was a necessity. Who would suppose or believe that days passed among fever wards and dying men, in a hospital away from the city, with no comforts and every privation, was voluntary! I dared not aspire to that!

Eugene says you mentioned something about black and white gingham at 4.50 a yard, but that I do not intend to give. I am going on a shopping expedition next week. I had to give fifty dollars a pair for leather shoes and what is worse wear them, with the thermometer at 96. I think prices are better for the purchaser here than anywhere else. I had quite a present yesterday. I had made a black cravat for Eugene and it was lying upon my table when Major Mason of the Army came in and took it, saying he wanted one. I let him keep it and a few hours afterwards he sent me five new novels and twenty pounds of coffee, telling me he knew I was too honest and scrupulous to drink the Hospital coffee. The only luxuries now that gentlemen can send me is tea and coffee and at the present rates his gift cost him over one hundred dollars. Shall I send you some?

I am sure I have not the slightest idea of what you mean when you say "Emma is learning something." Is anything wrong with her husband? As for Fanny's[15] engagement I do not wonder she broke it off, but only that it was on, he was such a dirty wriggling little tobacco chewer, she would prize a little notoriety much, from a morbid vanity and will not mature into any of the nobler attributes of womankind I think. Fanny Cohen makes no secret I believe of her partial engagement.

Do tell me if you ever heard of a young man named Napier Bartlett of the Washington Volunteers,[16] a very ugly but remarkably intelligent person, from New

15. Fanny Phillips, Phoebe's niece.
16. Napier Bartlett after the war wrote an account of his war experiences, published in New Orleans in 1874 under the title *A Soldier's Story of the War, Including the Marches and Battles of the Washington Artillery and of Other Louisiana Troops.*

Orleans. The reason I wish to know is that I met him casually and did him some little favors in the way of my profession which he seems very grateful for. He writes me very often, very clever shrewd rather brilliant letters from camp which I have not answered; and sends me books, one or two which he has written—one, a very pretty little novellette called "Claribel, a tale of the war." Please answer this as I am rather curious, fancying him rather a self made man.

If you are in earnest about being willing to preserve me some peaches if sugar was not so high, I should like a very small jar. I have over twenty pounds of sugar, being a part of my monthly rations, and I could either send it to you, or sell it for ten dollars a pound here and send you the money. I don't want many. If convenient please remember me. Thank dear Fanny a thousand times for her offer concerning her shawl, but tell her the Quarter Master General has promised to let me have some woollen cloth at government prices, as soon as any comes in; which will answer. I received her letter, and will answer soon. I wish I could see Lena's baby, is it really such a little beauty? I hope that she is pleased, she was always so anxious for it.

I must say goodbye as the Doctor has just come to lance a great abcess I have on my arm that has almost crazed me. You don't know how courageous the constant sight of amputations make one—you look upon anything less as trifling. Do give my kindest remembrances to all your household and write me soon. My greatest pleasure is the letters I get.

Sincerely yours

Phebe

My paper is miserable but I really cannot afford better, so will have to make up in agreeability for all defects.

CHAPTER 21

"I AM ALWAYS IN A HURRY"

Mrs. Gilmer
Care Major Gen. Gilmer
Charleston, S.C.

Chimborazo Hospital
20 October, 1863

I am divided, dear Lou, between the double duty and pleasure of writing to you and toasting coffee, as Candis is sick and Kate Ball gone to Charlotte in search of another brother who is reported slightly wounded.[1] Whatever I say or however stupid and complicated my epistle is, you will at least give me credit for my intentions. I was really desolée, as that term expresses, after you left, and besides mental affliction I had all sorts of misfortunes happen to me verily, my malignant star became in the ascendant.

I received a note from Lucy who I did not see till a few days ago telling me of your safe arrival and the adventurous visit you and Sallie made to Fort Sumter;[2] wishing to hear more of your warlike doings I paid a visit to sixth street. My first misfortune occurred there, as the ambulance as usual did not come for me in time, and I walked long after dark to my lonely room on Church Hill.

---

1. Candis is probably Mrs. C. Coffey, listed in returns of Chimborazo personnel at the National Archives as "ward matron," and assistant, along with Miss Kate Ball, to Phoebe Pember.
2. Gen. J. F. Gilmer, to whose wife this letter was written, had recently been ordered to Charleston to assist Beauregard in the defense of that city. See Jas. L. Nichols, *Confederate Engineers* (Tuscaloosa, 1957), 33.

Mrs. Stephens seemed delighted with having a home, and perfectly satisfied with everything around her. I passed the promised Saturday evening with her, and did not find the company as agreeable as it "was," I was careful to address all my pleasant commonplaces to the lady, and when "Walter" took me home was in a paroxysm of distress that we could not open the gate & some little detention was the result. However, I am simply malicious in saying these things, for *her* whole manner and conduct shows that she never thinks of that silly affair, and they are very kind, obliging people.[3]

Lucy wrote me that she had received a note from Mrs. "Accommodation" Long,[4] as she called her, in which she declines parting with any of those three petticoats upon any consideration whatever, so that financial scheme falls to the ground. She still thinks she will pay a visit to her husband.

I am preparing to go to my new room. Dr. *McCaw* sent me word to make use of the ambulance as it had to go to Market every morning, and a few squares farther would make no difference. This makes me more comfortable as from the prices charged me monthly I could not have afforded to engage the little carriage of the next division. On paying a visit to Mrs. Skinner I found that I was to have the *third* story, front room, no gas above the second story and no carpet in this bitter climate, and without light, fuel, or carpet I was to pay sixty dollars a month. She had told me that she did not want to make anything from her lodgers, that she had twelve rooms and paid eighteen hundred dollars a year, and I pledged myself

3. The reference is to Col. and Mrs. Walter H. Stephens. Col. Stephens, a graduate of the U. S. Military Academy, was engineer of the Richmond defenses. He and his wife, a resident of Louisiana at the time of their marriage, were former acquaintances of Mrs. Pember.
    4. Probably Mrs. Armistead L. Long.

under the circumstances to take one of the rooms. She asked me if I thought it was too much, and I said she was the best judge, and there the matter ended. I cannot say that I made much of a bargain.

I met Gen. Lawton[5] on the street, looking much stronger and better; he was on horseback; so I only had a word with him. How did you find your "lord and master" and did you give him the big apple? Mind that you go to Market Saturday evening in Charleston and buy some ground nut cake, and go and take a look at that elegant commencement of the new customs house.

I have but little news to tell you. Dr. H.[6] has forsworn the flesh pots of Egypt, and abjured the fascinations of the fair sex. He comes early to his Hospital and returns late. His avowed [?] purpose is to devote himself to the future happiness of his children and by way of insuring it he toots away at his flute all the leisure time he has, as when they attain the years of maturity he thinks they will stay at home to hear him play. He has secured the remains of my room at Mrs. McMinn, and asked permission to practice there. I could not refuse, but in going home found, then and since, a chair always put just in front of the looking glass so that he could practice the graces with the flute, and my soap and towels rung very wet. Since that time I have left one particular towel out for practicing purposes, and locked up my tooth brush, as a man with such saving propensities might take a "cheap brush" now and then, as it would cost him nothing.

I have all your Gospels safe and sound, presented to me by the Rev. Mr. Madison, a successor of Mr. Crooks. I

5. Lawton, who was disabled until May, 1863, from a wound received at Antietam, was made Quartermaster General in August, 1863. Well-educated and experienced as a railroad president, he supervised the Confederacy's quartermaster activities with commendable efficiency. His home was in Savannah, Ga.
6. Dr. S. E. Habersham, Surgeon-in-Charge of Mrs. Pember's Division.

will send them down to Major Reeves as soon as I can hear whether I can get you any straw for a hat. Peter offered me some money he said you left for milk, but as Dolan did not let me pay for that last month, or week, I declined to receive.

I have no news to tell you. Mrs. Randolph[7] has gone into the country with her husband to recruit his health, he looks most miserably, pale and of the consistency of white paper—unless she takes great care of him I do not think he will live long. I have never seen anyone so attentuated. Tell Ridgely I received an invitation from Miss Mary Gibson to spend the evening and sleep with her, both declined, and also a visit from Mr. David Forbes of two hours. Ask him if he is a fool, or only appears one. He tells me that the Yankees have caught Cary.

I really don't know what I am writing—it is one of my nervous days and a man in the next room has been bawling some information about a chicken that he got from Georgia that fought when "he cut off his wings and his spurs." I have heard "that chicken" now for one hour and have not a thought beyond.

Who shall I tell you about? Shirley is quite well I know you will be glad to hear, and getting a little stouter and my lips are also convalescent. He brought me a message from Mrs. Fitz. Lee,[8] begging me to come to see her as she was "in such wretched spirits and heard I was so pleasant." I told him that as soon as I got my cap and bells and my suit of Motley made I would go with pleasure. It is bad enough to have persons come to see you

7. Wife of Geo. W. Randolph, Confederate Secretary of War, March-November, 1862. He died of tuberculosis in 1867.

8. Probably Charlotte Lee, wife of Gen. W. H. F. ("Rooney") Lee, whose husband had been in Federal prison since June, 1863. She died in December 1863.

to be amused, but to be summoned to them for that purpose is more than my philosophy can stand.

Goodbye, *that chicken* is too much for me, combined with the loss of twenty dollars some one stole out of my purse and the scorching of the skirt you gave me, while I was stirring custard on the stove for a wounded man—it makes a concatination (*sic.*) of circumstances too hard to bear.

Give my love and a kiss (till I can give it myself) to Gen. Gilmer; tell him I shall only consider it a pleasure deferred. Most lovingly yours

Phebe

Do not be shocked at my paper

Mrs. Gilmer
Care Major Gen. Gilmer
Savannah, Ga.

Richmond, 30 December 1863

If I had written as often as I thought of you, dearest Lou, you would have been saturated with letters by this time, but I have had all sorts of accidents happen to me. First Kate Ball was telegraphed for to Columbia as her sister was very sick, and staid home a month, and then I got chills and fevers, that as soon as I got better left me with a stupid inert feeling that made me unfit for everything.

I have been thinking each day that I would see Gen. Gilmer & hear from him all concerning you, but although coming the end of each week, it still passes away without him. Mrs. Stevens has been expecting him weekly. I have not seen a great deal of her, as living in town I am always in a hurry to get in or out, but she paid me a visit announcing her *interesting* condition which she begged me to keep secret (which request I religiously observed till I found everybody was aware of the fact). They are both very nice kindhearted people and improve very much upon closer acquaintance.

Inquiries are very often made after you and the probability of your return to Richmond, and I sincerely hope that you and Sallie will soon be out. Gen. Lawton called to see me last Sunday night and told me he had secured Col. Myers's house and strange to say Mrs. Stevens had announced that very afternoon the same result in her favor. I need not say on whose side my sympathies leant.

My Hospital at present is quite empty—but has been very agreeable; made so by the presence of a dozen or more of young Baltimoreans, all gentlemen, but privates in the first Maryland, the "old Line." They were the Howards, Posts, Ridgely, etc.—and like all gentlemen were pleased and satisfied with everything I did for them. Since they have left, they have all written to me, kind warmhearted letters, and I have been overwhelmed by thanks for common services that have been paid fourfold to men a thousand times without even a recognition of them, all this has been very pleasant.

Chimborazo has changed a little, Stephen and Dr. Seabrook have had a quarrel which has been visited on the matron as the latter gentleman ignores my existence.[9] Shirley has neither been seen or heard from since the day after you left. The Medical Director sent him to Camp Lee, and the ungrateful fellow has not been near me,—at least at the Hospital, so your caution about the gay Lotharios of twenty two was thrown away. Report says he is engaged to the youngest Preston girl.

The Skinners are very nice people, and instead of a

9. Stephen was Dr. S. E. Habersham; Dr. E. M. Seabrook was a distinguished Confederate surgeon in charge of "Chimborazo Hospital No. 5."

boarder I am one of the family and a very pleasant family too.[10] The house is full of girls—Misses Stuart, Voss and Eliza Skinner. Col. Skinner is a very pleasant, well informed man, highly cultivated. He was educated in France, having been taken there when only nine years old by the Marquis Lafayette and brought up with his boys— they are Virginia all over, (which means that they would drive you crazy) kind hearted, generous, though very lazy, untidy people, who never have anything in its place or a place for anything, and who if they got hold of your dress by accident would just as likely put it on, always imploring you to do the same. If my room is more convenient for dressing or sleeping or talking, why in my room they all congregate and I am fortunate if no one carelessly mistakes my toothbrush for theirs—indeed I carry it in my pocket for fear of accidents.

It seemed to me I lived a week during the twenty four hours which constituted Christmas. On the eve I was invited to Mrs. Randolph's and found all married people there, and more than I should have gone to meet had I known of it. The evening was not very agreeable, though Stephen was there, Mrs. Haxall was loud in her lamentations that two such *nice* people, who would make such a *nice* match did not appear to appreciate each other. We did not get away till past midnight and by eight the next morning I was on my way to prepare for the important day. We made twenty four gallons of Egg-Nogg inviting *all* in the whole Division to come and drink and gave to each a good sized cake. At two o'clock having roasted a dozen turkeys and seven gallons of oysters we shared them out and hoped that each man got his share. After all this was accomplished, I had the kitchen table carried into

10. Family of Col. Frederick Skinner, 1st Virginia Infantry, whom Mrs. Burton Harrison in *Recollections Grave and Gay*, p. 79, characterizes as "that picturesque old warrior and fire-eater."

my little room, a personal turkey with all new accompaniaments sett out and then sent for the poor outcast Marylanders to come and dine. Presided at the table of ten, caring for them, left them at five and dressed for a great dinner at Col. Skinner's, for with true Virginia hospitality they had not only invited me, but requested me to fill the two vacant chairs by my side. I took Dr. Baylor and John Eagen Howard, had dinner at seven, and went by invitation at ten to Dr. Gibson's to see the Christmas tree on which I found my Christmas gift pretty enough to be most acceptable and simple enough to preclude all feelings of obligation.[11]

I need not ask you if this was not very pleasant for I know what you would feel if you were the actor in the scene, but the kindness and attention I meet with are very gratifying and go far to reconcile your loss, which is saying a great deal, for you do not know, dearest Lou, the love and regard I feel for you. I am not a responsive or demonstrative person and am very apt to *chill* any open expression of this kind but one feels it all the same. Perhaps if I have merited any reward in this world it may be given me in the shape of a power to prove this.

The Virginia women are annoying me again and absolutely came into my sanctum with their pipes. I remonstrated with one who expressed surprise that I should object to a pipe, asking where I was born. I answered So. Ca. whereupon she composedly removed the obnoxious article and remarked drily, "Well, she was always a nasty, rampagious little hussy." I did not take the application but told her to go.

So Lucy received her Christmas gift at last. I saw her the

11. Dr. Charles Bell Gibson and his family lived on Gibson Street. Mrs. Burton Harrison described the home as "a haunt of clever and responsive people." *Recollections Grave and Gay,* 159. Dr. Baylor was probably Dr. J. C. Baylor, who was assigned to one of the Richmond hospitals.

day before making a plenteous meal, and looking quite robust, although they are all very near me I do not see much of them for though I have all the inclination still these things must be mutual.

Stephen's mind has been much exercized of late and his love trouble still continues. His attentions are distracted between Jinny Pollard at Mrs. Randolph, Carrie Stuart at Mrs. Skinner's and Alice Macgill. I meet him very often out in society and at last he deigned to pay me a formal visit. I neither asked to be excused or prepared to go down to him, but simply said "Very well" when the servant announced the fact, and went to bed—this was repeated three times. How long he staid and who entertained him, I am still ignorant of. He is at present in a very indignant mood in some reports about his courting researches and informed me this morning that he intended visiting but at three houses, Mrs. Jones, Randolph and Harrison's, unless "Mrs. Gilmer comes when I shall extend my visits to her house"—allow me to be the first to congratulate you.

Your neighbors the Crenshaws had a great party last night with full band of music. I got my information from Kate Ball who still lives opposite. I can give you no information concerning Church Hill. My Hospital neighbor Mrs. Tschusli [?] has lost her only child, a very fine boy of eleven years old and I feel the greatest sympathy for her—he was only ill for three days with Scarlet Fever.

The President holds his first general leveé on the first of January to which I hear everybody and his wife are going, there being a great many persons of high social position who have never seen him. In Congress they are fighting the financial question. Mr. Lyons[12] (who I met at Mrs. Jones) told me they intended taxing the people over

12. Probably James Lyons, Confederate Congressman from Virginia.

ten millions of dollars and were determined to try and raise the depreciated currency.

It is blowing a perfect hurricane of wind, sleet and rain, and I fear the weather will prevent the charitable ladies of Richmond from fulfilling their intention of carrying round a New Years dinner to the Hospitals. I had no funds for my Christmas dinner, but raised them by condemning old comforts and blankets and having them sold, adding all donations received from private individuals among which was thirty dollars from Sally Lawton, should you see her tell her how I appreciated it. Dr. McCaw came in during the day and had all the arrangements explained to him, he laughed heartily and said I was a monstrous humbug, but seemed very much pleased.

Good bye, pray forgive my miserable ink. I could not get anything better, although I remembered how delicate your sight is. I cannot even see to read this over it is so late and stormy. Give my love to Mrs. Porter and a kiss to Sally. I am still in hopes of congratulating *the* General myself, in my own way.

I hope that we may soon meet for I long to see you and almost feel sentimental about it, so with much love, most affectionately yours,

Phebe Y. P.

CHAPTER 22

"EVERY GIRL IN RICHMOND IS ENGAGED OR ABOUT TO BE"

Mrs. Gilmer
Care Major Gen. J. F. Gilmer
Savannah, Ga.

Chimborazo Hosp. 19th Feb. 1864

Dearest Lou,

You were so good answering my letter so soon that I cannot help replying immediately to yours received yesterday without, however, having anything very special to say. I hope that I may be able to hold my pen, for the thermometer is only ten degrees below Zero, the river hard frozen, and my early walk from Franklin St. over that bridge (not of sighs) of winds was anything but thawing. My hands feel stiff even now. As for being either useful or ornamental [during] this spell, I give up the attempt; it is even hard to keep clean, all the water being ice.

I saw Lucy and the baby: both very pretty, though the style of bringing up already would make your hair stand on end. It has half a dozen regular nurses and any number of irregular ones. I flatter myself that I rescued it from suffocation from the warmth and weight of six blankets and other comfortable things one mild evening. It is very pretty and has a very healthy way of crying. I have seen Major Alexander very often lately on the subject of a

182

pair of cavalry boots, having a new pvt. in the Maryland cavalry who has none. He is only eighteen but unfortunately requires as much leather as thirty would. You see I can afford to be generous now as I am the wealthy possessor of three thousand a year, Dr. McCaw having announced that important fact to me yesterday. Are you not happy to hear that my country thus recognizes my important services.

We are rather hard up at the Hospital, as the $1.25 cards barely feeds the men. Congress has doubled the allowance but the law does not take effect for a month. In the meantime we do our best to prevent dissatisfaction. We are now a Maryland hospital at my particular request. The Virginians are not kind in feeling and act to their sister state (like the Georgians to So. Ca.) and so my love of equity and justice was aroused and I have taken them all (I suppose I must not say to my bosom) under my protecting wing. For the first time I feel the sweets of gratitude, and Mr. Henry Warfield of Baltimore, who came in to negotiate the exchange of Gen. Trimble for White, told me that my name was a household word in Baltimore—which is very agreeable.

I pass the house every morning, sometimes see Peter and the General's horse, which looks very well, and one day Dr. Baylor and I (who have joined company to walk out in the morning) drove Thaddeus all the way home from a vicinity very near the Market. We saw him safely home before we left him. Of Col. and Mrs. Stevens I do not see much, they were very kind in professions and offers, but to speak plainly as I always do to you, there is more talk than anything else. Her transactions are too clever for me, and I am not quite up to her management.

Mr. Crenshaw I have seen getting into his buggy on crutches and very lame from severe rheumatism, and there is no Church Hill news at all. When the Yankee prisoners escaped there was a guard placed around Mrs. Van Lon's [?] house and grounds. The Confederate government was too delicate minded to search the premises. In spite of all your disbelief Mrs. Skinner is as good as gold, which is very good in these days, and the house is more like a home than any I could have found. If through wrong judgement or any other reason she charged me too much, she certainly makes up for it in other ways, and I make over to her as much again as I pay to equalize matters. I could not be more pleasantly situated. Sallie Lawton's house is almost three squares from Mrs. Skinner's, the first being the corner of 8th and Marshall, the latter of 6th and Franklin, so that she is quite accessible. I took her a package of marrow, prepared in a cake to send you; it was not as much as I would have liked to collect, but being Lent, Stephen finds that it does not compart with his Christianity to eat anything but Hospital cornbread and marrow. By the by he is getting more pious, and meanness & religion seem in his case to go hand in hand. He says he has given up tobacco to be enabled to save what he spent on that article to give to the widows and orphans. I don't know what *they* get but I do know that he levies blackmail upon every man he comes across for smoking and chewing purposes, and there has been a general improvement in this hospital, every man by his own account having "no tobacco." Between the necessity of doing his duty and his fear of his superior officers he is generally in a pitiable state. I have no idea that he will remain in a state proper to control a hospital three months longer—but no wonder that when the stomach is kept so heavy, the brain gets light. He is the smallest of mortals.

Of the gaiety I am not competent to write, having

borne a part in only one of the entertainments and then feeling out of place—so much so that I retired for the season. If Spartan austerity is to win our independence, we are a lost nation. I do not like the signs, and fear the writing on the wall might in time come to us. Now the community are alive on this as yet mischievous finance bill. For two days we have been unable to purchase anything, no one understanding the technicalities and fearful under the circumstances of losing some advantage. Even when willing to sell, the difficulty of change presents itself, small bills being at a premium. I read the bill, commencing carefully, feeling the responsibility devolving on me as the holder of *five one hundred dollar bills,* and before I got to the second clause I gave up as quietly as Martin Scott's corn, and "came down."

Can I get a piece of black and white gingham in Savannah? If I can at seven or eight dollars a yard will you buy the whole piece for me, and write me to that effect. I want the plaid equal, it washes so well, and cannot get any in Richmond. Perhaps they have it in the wholesale store there, as they are apt to buy that description of goods for the southern market. I have not received any straw that was promised but will make another effort. I *did* try a couple of months after you left, and then gave it up, but will stir Dr. V. on the subject.

My best love to *the general* and remembrances to Mrs. Porter and the girls.

Most affectionately yours
P. Y. P.

I have to commence another sheet to tell you that the reason my paper is so dirty is because Kate Ball stirred the fire all out upon my carpet and snatched up my epistle as being the nearest thing to pick up the coals. I cannot stop to re-write it, for the days are very short, and I have a great deal to do, gentlemen being more troublesome than other people. I did not tell you of my trip a week ago. I received an invitation from the Maryland Line to go to Hanover Junction and dine with them as they had stolen a Pig and two Hens. The inviters were Company C. and Mrs. Swan of Baltimore went with me. We had a very pleasant time,—a great deal of hand shaking and many compliments, arrived there at ten and left at four. Unfortunately, my old prisoner, a nervous headache, attacked me and I was put to bed in the Col's tent till the Ambulance could be got. At the Depot I am sorry to say I tumbled out and made rather a display, but there is a bright side to all pictures, I had on nice cotton stockings and new shoes and any woman in the Confederacy with such luxuries can afford to show her legs. A more substantial proof of regard from Maryland came in the shape of a dozen pair of black kid gloves, but unfortunately they got lost, or cannot be traced. There are so many inducements for dishonesty in these days that it is never safe to trust any one.

Do try and get the gingham for me; by saying I want it in equal parts I mean I want the black and white equally divided, as I find it is the only plaid that will wash, and write and tell me if you succeed as I am looking out every day for the same.

This wheat question is a fearful one. Almost all the bakeries in the city are closed, and I cannot get my principal means of subsistence—biscuits. My point has been gained on the ration question—we no longer receive them and I am delivered from Bacon, Room rent, wood, flour & all the attendant evils—the commutation being fixed at 250 dollars the month. At first they fixed the allowance at a dollar and a quarter a day but as that did not buy a pound of flour the wise heads of the nation saw their mistake.

Every girl in Richmond is engaged or about to be. Cooper DeLeon[1] addressed Miss Truxey Johnson who responded amicably but the Papa questioned him on his belief in the Trinity and he not responding reasonably according to Mr. Johnson's belief the old gentleman objected. It will be a new feature introduced in love affairs if the final "parient" puts the lover through the catechism. By the by, Stephen teaches the poor children every Friday night, but I am afraid that this will not give him Brandon. I think he has a hankering after that lively retreat, and Miss Belle is a teacher. Mrs. James Caskie came out to see me at the Hospital some weeks since. Is this one your friend?

With love, yours   P.Y.P.

---

1. T. C. DeLeon, journalist, and author of *Belles, Beaux and Brains of the 60's, Four Years in Rebel Capitals* (Mobile, 1890) and other works.

CHAPTER 23

"THE FIGHTING IS SO NEAR"

Mrs. J. F. Gilmer
Savannah, Ga.

Chimborazo Hosp.

16 April, 1864

I have been asking after you, dearest Lou, till I have determined whether I owe you a letter or not (a point I have forgotten) to find out when we are to see you, for your coming is like a royal progress in its uncertainty. Every morning that I pass Mrs. Stevens I hear your hens cackling and it almost breaks my heart to think of the fresh eggs that ought to be invigorating "the General," swallowed by the Stevens dynasty. The Spring is behaving beautifully and awaiting you with dry eyes and open arms, and so are *we!* that is, Stephen and I!!!

I am very much distressed to hear about Gen. Gilmer's eyes, and only hope that nature may help herself or the oculist be mistaken in part as they so often are, for I think less is known of that delicate organ than any other part of the human system. You know the general health affects the eyes so much, and the constant excitement he has lived in lately, with imperiled bodily health may go far to produce temporary weakness of sight. I think any affection of the eyes the greatest defermation one can suffer from, particularly with an active mind and industrious habits. However, while this lasts Gen. Gilmer will only act as usual, seeing through your eyes, which are pretty sharp. I do long to see you both.

All Chimborazo has been broken up except my Division to which all the old Hospital rats and sorebacks and grumblers have been sent, including three crazy men—one of whom has a chronic affection for pulling off all his clothes the moment I go into his Ward; perhaps the poor fellow has had to strip himself for the visiting Doctor and don't know the difference. Anticipating the crowd I did all I could to make Stephen prepare but whenever I came across him he was turning round like a tee—to turn as each new requirement struck against his brain. Just as I supposed he stuffed all my requisitions into his pocket, just as he usually stuffs all my good things in the same neighborhood, and when bright and early Monday morning, with six hundred patients on my hands and no bed clothing, or liquor, or rags or anything else I went to seek him, he could not be found, after there had been a hue and cry for an hour, in walked Stephen, beaming! Light irradiated from his smiling face, and soft delight sweetened his bland tones—as he asked me to walk over to his office—he had been driving all morning round the point and to Ruckets with "a grand-daughter of Patrick Henry—Mrs. Clark—formerly a Miss Bruce—immensely wealthy people." Fortunately anger made me speechless, and when I did find my voice it was only to say I had not time to play the agreeable to Patrick Henry's descendant. However, he did bring her over to my kitchen where she asked a blessing upon my undertaking and I responded by spilling a cup of cream over her new black bombazine dress.

I saw Lucy for the first time for a long while three evenings since. Lucy has never been to see me since I went to live a stones throw from her, and occupied as I was I really did not feel that all the politeness should come from me. I was not at all offended but as I never saw any of the family I had no visits to return. Mrs. Stevens I cannot take to, for I do not believe in her, or in him either. Their attentions are all invested and *not* in four per cents either—they are expected to bear better interest.

Sallie Lawton has been very unwell, she says, tho' I have only seen her twice—once when I went for her girls to spend the day with me at the hospital and another time when I went after tea. She cannot come to see me after dark as she has no escort & I am not at home any other time. By evening I am too weary to dress and go out to visit if even I had some one always to go with me.

There is a hum of expectation pervading the air in Richmond and flying rumors of an advance. Longstreet at Charlottesville—Beauregard at Petersburg and Polk in the Valley, they say. Even the assistant surgeons have been required to hold themselves in readiness to move at a moment's warning. I have strong presentiments that the coming struggle will end the war. Our men appear to be so hopeful and there is such a vacillating and bombastic style about our enemies—their efforts seem more spasmodic than well sustained. All the returned prisoners, of whom I see a great many, tell wonderful tales of how well they have been treated. Gen. Bragg has been putting his fingers in the Hospital pies and referring [to] abuses when none existed,[1] closing them and dispersing all the corps just when the spring campaign is about to open. Major Norris is displaced. Thad. Myers spent a day with me and represented my appearance and health as in such a precarious state that sister immediately sent for me to go to Savannah to her. This is a great act for dear sister

1. General Braxton Bragg on Feb. 24, 1864 was made principal military adviser to President Davis.

for she has always been a most devoted daughter and the acceptance of such a proposition would raise a storm about her head. If we are to meet I fear that it will be as great potentates do, on neutral ground. I am really sick I fear, having constant pains in my side and chest and profuse night sweats. The constant change from a very hot kitchen to the cold air without and going in and out sick wards very much heated, all day & every day may be the cause. Perhaps this unvarying routine for seventeen months without a day of rest which is part of Nature's dispensation will in time tell on my constitution.

Church Hill is not behaving very well, as many young ladies are enjoying single blessedness with the painful accompanyments of married life. I often meet Miss Green (Miss Eliza I mean) with sundry plates and napkins going to be invested in some neighboring ten per cent paying Bank. I am sure that you will have no trouble with the servants on your return they will be so glad to see you, and perhaps painful experiences will make them wise.

I hear that Mrs. Stannard is dubious about fulfilling the marriage contract with Mr. Souleé and still reflects about the matter.[2] Gen. Randolph is entirely restored to health. Mr. Memminger is now a neighbor of yours but I hope you will not cultivate him to any great extent.[3] What about my gingham? I can get a piece here for twelve dollars a yard, shall I take it or can you do better for me —please write me a line as the season is advancing and it takes me some time to get a dress done now—if I cannot

2. Probably Mrs. Robert Stanard and Pierre Soule. In *Recollections Grave and Gay,* pp. 159-160, Mrs. Burton Harrison states: "I think we all fancied that Mrs. Robert Stanard came nearer to realizing the French ideal of a salon than any other hostess in Richmond. She was a widow, reputed wealthy and of considerable personal distinction, handsome, dark-eyed, and wondrously persuasive with the other sex. . . . At Mrs. Stanard's one saw much of Pierre Soule. . . ."

3. C. G. Memminger, Confederate Secretary of the Treasury Feb. 1861-July 1864.

get it cheaper in Savannah then it is no use troubling you. Give my love to Mrs. Porter and say how glad I am to hear that the morphine is doing her good though I hope it will not permanently affect her gaiety and in time make her a hum-drum old woman which nature never intended her to be. Give dear little Luly a kiss for me, and for yourself and Gen. Gilmer I send all the love and sympathy I have been keeping waiting—

Most affectionately yours
P.Y.P.

Chimborazo Hosp. Richmond.
22 June, 1864

I have waited and waited, dearest Lou, and whenever I passed old Briggs' looked out like sister Anne, and all for naught, for not only have you *not* come, but I do not believe that you are coming. I really think that both yourself and "the General" are of too much importance actually to give yourselves a false value by disappointing people in this way, like that other General — Tom Thumb or the Irish giant. This thing has been carried so far that I actually met Peter with the market basket, preparing for your Sunday dinner and all the while you are quietly vegetating up to your ankles in sand.

You do not know what you have missed. Richmond has been delightful. Today is the first warm weather, *and* for the last three weeks there has been no day or night that the booming of cannon has not been the last sound at night and the first in the morning—while none are to be seen of the masculine kind but couriers, wounded soldiers and a few surgeons, except at times when whole squads or even a division as Picketts did—march through to reinforce or change position. One night I was awak-

ened by the tramp or rather clatter of five thousand cavalry, silently filing through Franklin Street by the light
of a very waning moon.[4]

As you may suppose, my Hotel is very, very full, most
of the convalescing boarders sleeping upon the floor. The
fighting is so near that in some cases the wounded are
brought in from four to five hours after the engagement.
I have now over six hundred and am very much worn
out, for there is no rest, not even a Sabbath day, & never
having been absent one single day since you left I begin to
flag a little, feeling the absolute necessity of change of
some kind. Besides this constant labor of mind and body
there are other matters to trouble me. The Hospital is half
Virginian and half Maryland and the jealousy is great, so
that there is a constant fuss. If I show kindness to a man
who is a Marylander the Virginians stir up some complaint and vice versa, while Stephen listens to the last
comer & makes foolish rules that annoy everybody. By the
by he has grown very peculiar—does not visit anywhere,
not even at Mrs. Harrison's, and is miserably thin and
dreary, in fact has lost his looks, his flesh, his friends, his
sweethearts, in fact everything but his appetite—*that*
"undismayed o'er every ruin smiles." Fanny Cohen wrote
me that he was engaged to Phebe Elliott, but of course
that is an absurdity.

I see and meet everybody on Franklin Street. Mrs.
Randolph is still very attentive, and knowing how very
variable she is I am not much there. I see a great deal of
the Gibsons and find the Doctor *when he pleases* to be—
charming. Mrs. Stannard invited me to breakfast but
something prevented. She went quite into ecstasies over

---

4. The shifting of Confederate forces through Richmond to which Mrs.
Pember here refers was to repel the threat in the Petersburg area posed by
Grant's movement south of the James River which was begun on June 14.
Beauregard's masterful defense, and the arrival of reenforcements from Lee,
prevented a Federal break-through on June 18.

the charms of your father. I had no idea that he was a lady killer. I see more of the Grattans than formerly, they are so amiable that there is no use in feeling hurt with them and Sally and I have entered into a calf skin speculation, commencing with the expectation of getting four pairs out of our hundred dollar skin and going up to a dozen after minute measuring. Mrs. Sallie looks very well and is very comfortably paid. I have seen her too, very often and had the pleasure of a visit of a whole day from little Sally and Alick.[5] I heard Sallie imparting to Candis (for they fraternized instantly) that *"never, never* in the *whole* of her life did she and Alick have enough to eat,"* and have a dim recollection, for I was very busy, of an indignant remark of Candis about "what sort of unhuman people their ma and pa must be" and of a table set out under a tent I have in the yard, and Sally and Alick seated in a land flowing with milk and honey. I hope sincerely that they are both alive, and feel that I did my duty for I spoke very sharply to Candis, who has got quite beyond my control—however, as I was obliged to go in the Wards, Kate tells me she said, she wasn't going to have the starving of any poor child on her soul, when her day came.

I think that you had better give up the straw as a bad job, as Dr. Veiden says the enemy are in possession of the country where the plaiter lives. I see beautiful hats from South Carolina made from palmetto and hope that your prejudices will not interfere with Luly's comfort; because they cannot be made in Georgia.

Mrs. Stevens has located herself in the most comfortable house on Church Hill, free of all the labors of housekeeping and as far as I know, perhaps of many other

5. Doubtless Mrs. A. R. Lawton and her two children are the persons to whom Mrs. Pember here refers.

things. From her disappearance on the porch I fancy an olive branch has sprouted. She has been very hearty and active—but "Walter" is with Gen. Lee.[6]

The marvelous girl, Tiny, comes over with flowers for the soldiers;—she is really growing very pretty, and is au fait as to all the people on the Hill their comings and goings. Mrs. Long also expects, but came up from Petersburg in an open buggy without any back upon receipt of the news of the first fight, thinking that Gen. Long might be wounded. She was sick at the Spotswood so I felt sorry for her and went to see her, sat some time and left with Dr. Garnett. She begged me to have Gen. Long taken to my Division should he be wounded and in my promising to do so and nurse him faithfully, she asked if in that case *she* could not occupy my little chamber or office. Was not that natural?

Your friend Mrs. Caskie has been out two or three times to see me, but I cannot keep up anything like visiting. I am so weary by night time. We have officers now as Dr. Reed's[7] hospital is broken up in consequence of gangrene breaking out. It is true that he has taken the Poor house but in the mean time the officers have got scattered. I find in all the cases I have met with that they have been rougher than the men.

Give my love to Gen. Gilmer and tell him that I am waiting very anxiously to congratulate him only fearing that he will forget all about it before I have a chance. Goodbye. I am so tired I hardly know what nonsense I am writing. Please send and tell me when you arrive.—truly

P.Y.P.

---

6.   Col. Walter H. Stevens was ordered to report to Beauregard on June 14 to assist in the defense of Petersburg. He was subsequently made Chief Engineer of the Army of Northern Virginia (a position he had previously held for a time) and on Aug. 28, 1864, was promoted to brigadier general.

7.   Probably Dr. James B. Read, of Savannah, Georgia, whose operations in Richmond during the war attracted much favorable attention. See Cunningham, *Doctors in Gray*, pp. 225, 232, 236.

INDEX

Amputations: 106-108

Ball, Kate ("Miss G."): 93, 110, 138, 165, 172, 176, 180, 185

Baltimore, Maryland, under Federal occupation: 162-163

Bartlett, Napier: 170-171

Bragg, Gen. Braxton, interferes in hospital affairs: 190

Butler, Gen. Benjamin F.: 3

Chimborazo Hospital, burying the dead: 99-100; celebration of Christmas: 178-179; description of: 4-10; diet: 30-35, 69-70, 82-84, 107, 155; diversions of wounded: 105-106; equipment: 28-29, 43, 47, 54, 55-56, 67, 83-84, 193; evacuation of: 127-128; finances: 183; furloughs: 95-96; ice houses: 34; nurses' quarters: 153; occupation by Federals: 134, 137-144; organization of: 23-24, 27-28, 58, 60, 189; visiting at: 13, 91-95.

Clothing, in Richmond: 155, 161, 163, 170-171, 185-186, 191-192.

Confederate prisoners, care at Chimborazo: 97-99.

Davis, Jefferson, departure of family from Richmond, 130; leaves church on receipt of Confederate defeat at Petersburg: 128; to hold open house, 180

Davis, Mrs. Jefferson, gossip about: 149-150, 154-155, 160

Death, reaction of wounded: 45-47, 67-68

DeLeon, T. C.: 3

Federal prisoners, food: 89-90, 98-99

Freeman, Douglas Southall: 2, 5

Gilmer, Col. Jeremy F.: 153, 157; promoted and sent to Charleston, S. C.: 166-167

Gilmer, Mrs. Jeremy F., letters to, 172-192

Greenhow, Mrs. Rose O'neal: 151

Habersham, Dr. Stephen E.: 165, 174, 177-178, 180, 184, 193

Health, of soldiers in the field: 123

Hollywood Cemetery, Richmond, 100

Hopkins, Mrs. Arthur F., criticism of, 157

Hospitals, civilian contributions to: 58-60; Confederate military: 23; matrons: 24

"Hospital Rats": 12, 28, 139, 140

Inflation: 15

Johnston, Mrs. Joseph E.: 150

Key, Francis Scott: 99

Key, Richard Hammond, death and burial of: 99-100

197